The Candid Odyssey

Exploring India and the

Philosophy of Life

B. Johny

The Candid Odyssey: Exploring India and the Philosophy of Life

Author
B. Johny
www.bjohny.com

All stories, incidents, and events mentioned in this book are true and based on the author's personal experiences during his solo journey across India.

Publisher
Notion Press

For the seekers.

Day 0

There is a period in our lives when we fall to the bottom and don't know how to get up. It is the period when we fail hard and lose faith in ourselves; the time when we feel stuck and don't know what to do next. The tough times of our lives. I also went through this when my ambitious business plans failed miserably after putting in more than three years of genuine hard work. Potential acquisitions were turned down at the last moment, new ideas practically didn't work out, my savings were depleted, I became depressed, my family lost faith in me, and eventually, I lost myself. It was tragic. In such times, we can either stay lost, keep persevering, or leave everything behind and reinvent ourselves. Staying lost isn't going to do any good, so it's better not to follow that route. At the same time, I have persevered a lot and reached a point where I hate what I do. Can't persevere anymore. So, only one option remains: self-discovery.

Self-discovery is about trying to answer the fundamental questions of life: Who are we? What is the purpose of life? How should we live? These are some of the toughest questions in the world, with no well-defined answers—questions for which some dedicate their lifetimes seeking answers. Some learn from spiritual leaders, others gain insights from experience, some read scriptures, and some meditate. I, too, considered connecting the dots from my past, consulting psychologists, and taking a break from everything. The last one—taking a break—felt the most interesting. A break from all problems, worries, and failures. An opportunity to look into others' lives, gain various perspectives, and ultimately find more clarity about life. A journey to explore new places, new cultures, new experiences, and, most importantly, a new self. That journey is this eight-week-long solo trip across India.

It takes two to three weeks to create a plan and prepare for the journey. At a high level, India is classified into seven regions, with one week planned for exploring each region. An extra week is also included for contingencies, making a total of eight weeks. That's all for the itinerary; everything else is decided on the go. In terms of money, I have around 70,000 rupees. To put this in perspective, that's the price of a decent laptop in India. No other savings or investments—just that much. For luggage, a cheap 65 L rucksack is ready. The luggage includes six t-shirts, three pairs of pants, one raincoat, a small 10 L backpack, a pair of flip-flops, necessary medicines, pepper spray (better safe than sorry), and some essential tools and accessories like scissors, a power bank, a water bottle, a wallet, a phone, and a charger. In total, the luggage weighs around 10 kg. Packing completed successfully!

Now it's time to overcome the biggest challenge: convincing my family. I haven't been a traveler before, and as you can expect, my family members resisted. Their main arguments were, "You haven't done anything like this; it's dangerous to travel alone; we can't help you in case of an emergency," and many more. But, as decided earlier, there would be no turning back. After a few days of strong disagreements, they agreed to two weeks of travel. At least it will get the trip started—that's more important. So, everything is set. From now on, it's us. You and me. Together, we will explore India and the philosophy of life. Hope you are ready :)

Day 1

We are starting from Ernakulam in Kerala and will be going to Coimbatore in Tamil Nadu by train. These are the southern parts of

India, almost. Since it's the first day, we have no idea what to expect on this journey, but it feels incredibly exciting nonetheless! From the open windows of the train, we can see rural houses, green paddy fields, calm rivers, small forests, rocky hills, and much more. It's all beautiful. We can also spot lots of playful monkeys and shy peacocks along the way. As we reach Coimbatore, we notice small houses with similar square-shaped structures, adorned in a variety of stunning colors. When we see them from afar, the combined beauty of geometry and color captivates us. It continues until we reach the Coimbatore railway station. Thanks to Indian Railways for offering affordable travel options across the country; most of our journey will be by train. We will come across many railway stations and train memories. We will book our tickets online, usually 2-3 days before each ride. And of course, we will try our best every time to get a window seat! :)

Having arrived in Coimbatore by afternoon, we head to our accommodation on Raja Street. As you know, we are on a tight budget. We can only spend around 1,000 rupees per day on everything, including travel, food, and accommodation. So, we will be staying in the cheapest accommodations we can find, costing around 300 rupees per night. We book these rooms online once we reach the destination. After reaching the room, we keep the big rucksack there, take some necessary items in the small backpack, and then go out. That's the process. Ready to head out?

Coimbatore is known for its markets, textiles, industries, and history. There aren't many attractions here; it's the place itself that's the attraction. We can take a leisurely stroll along the Smart City walkway near Valankulam Lake. It's like a couple's area, full of couples everywhere, young and old. While some are chatting with ice creams, others are trying their best to take pictures with the lake in the frame. Click! With the calm lake beside us, we lie on a slab, resting under a tree as we reflect on what we're doing here. Like all deep thinking, it will probably lead to a good nap. :) And it's not just us; we have a few rats for company as well. By the way, vehicles are bustling on the road beside the walkway, so the nap doesn't last long. As we walk further, we can find the bustle in Raja and Vysial streets in the evening nerve-wracking. There are a lot of shops and street vendors on both sides of the road, filled with shoppers, vehicles, and even cows! What's even more interesting is that large buses navigate right through all of this, of course, without hitting anything. Everything is in harmony. We roam around those streets without even checking the maps while also enjoying some street food along the way. Cut fruits, omelets, juice, and more. Anyway, by around 10 pm, we quit wandering. :)

As we go through all of this, we experience a lot of happiness. If we reflect on what truly made us happy, it wasn't any luxury or success. It's just the small moments we experienced: the old couples trying hard to take pictures with proper poses, the rats playing hide and seek near the tree we slept under, the way the bus maneuvers through the bustling street, the taste of an inexpensive omelet served on a leaf, and more. All such moments and encounters are a pure source of happiness. But we somehow forget to notice, comprehend, and feel them. Happiness is everywhere; we just need to look carefully. :)

Day 2

Usually, we stay around one day per destination, but certain days will be just continuous travel. Today is such a day—an all-day travel day. Coimbatore feels so calm in the early morning. At least the buses are now moving freely through the streets, and the shops haven't opened yet. Before the city wakes up, we need to leave for Mettupalayam, which is a connecting bus station for our actual destination, Coonoor. It's a bit of a struggle to find the right buses because the signboards are in Tamil only; nothing is written in English or Hindi anywhere. We have to ask around five people to find the right bus, using gestures more than words. This is a fun challenge we'll encounter often in many regions. Why? Because India is home to over 100 languages! Yes, that's far more than we can handle. :)

On the bus, we notice a middle-aged man who appears to be somewhat mentally unwell. He starts making noise and causing trouble for the passengers beside him. While some people understand the situation and try to remain patient, not everyone is so forgiving. A few passengers stop the bus and begin questioning, scolding, and even assaulting him. In the end, we see someone pushing him out of the bus! The rest is unknown. Some may find it brave, but it's outrageous. Imagine if we were that person who got pushed out of the bus. What would we feel? Before we do or say something to someone, if we ask ourselves how the other person feels, we will know what's right and what's wrong. Empathy is the foundation of our actions toward others.

Coonoor is a hill station. Yes, we are going up! The bus journey is wonderful, with lots of hairpin bends along the way. Hundreds of monkeys line the roadside, playing, eating, and grooming each other. Many of them look to us for food as the bus passes by. Sorry, monkeys, but we don't have any bananas! :) The lush green trees and the morning sun provide us with a serene view throughout the bus trip. It's getting colder, though. As we reach Coonoor, we are welcomed by a unique mix of rain and fog. It's fascinating to see how both work together. Steam locomotives are quite rare now, and operating them on top of mountains certainly qualifies it as a UNESCO World Heritage site. It will take us to Ooty on a one-and-a-half-hour ride through the hills, surrounded by scenic trees. Hundreds of eucalyptus trees packed together beside the track provide splendid views. The distant hills, homes and markets dotting the valley, and the beauty of Ooty all make the train ride fascinating. Those desktop wallpapers we used to admire in childhood are becoming a reality now! :) The train runs very slowly; even walking could be much faster. But it's the slowness that makes the train ride so enjoyable. Sometimes, it is better to enjoy the slowness, right? How we cope with circumstances changes the actual impact of the same!

Ooty is a small town and hill station that offers stunning views of tea gardens and a pleasant climate. That's not all; we can also stroll around the lake and the flower gardens. As time passes, the cold gets much colder now. We also need to go, so we'll get on another bus, to Gudalur. It is also part of the Nilgiri Mountains, associated with the Western Ghats. The journey offers good views, a forest vibe, and mists along the way. We can also find fresh carrots for sale by the roadside as the bus stops in between. That's our food! :) From Gudalur, we are going to Kozhikode. It's raining heavily, and the bus is almost empty. Late at night, we arrive in Kozhikode and stroll through the vibrant city, passing Sweetmeat Street, a culturally significant walking street. However, the market is mostly empty, likely due to the rain and our late arrival. We can't help but notice a few suspicious looks from some people. To avoid any trouble, let's make our way to the railway station quickly, as our train will be departing soon.

Tonight, we are going to sleep on the train. Usually, if a train journey lasts longer than six hours, we will take the Sleeper Class at night. This way, we can save a lot of time and accommodation costs for that night.

So, expect this strategy to be reused many times as we go further! :) We also need to take many precautions while sleeping on the train, such as using the rucksack as our pillow, keeping our phone and wallet hidden in the rucksack, keeping the pepper spray in our pockets, and, of course, being more vigilant. We need to take risks, but not foolish ones. That's why precautions are important. Remember, it's better to be safe than sorry. Oh, didn't say where we are going next. We'll see tomorrow! :)

Day 3

We are in a deep sleep, even though it's our first train-sleeping experience on this journey. The tea sellers and the train horns wake us up early in the morning, and they surely will, no matter how sleepy you are. The first thing we do is check if we've lost any of our belongings. This isn't just for today; we continue this ritual throughout the journey. Anyway, today, we are going to Goa. The train glides through the scenic Konkan zone, offering beautiful hill views and numerous tunnels. It's a fascinating journey. Each time we pass through a tunnel, we feel a sense of joy, knowing that at the end of the darkness lies light. Witnessing that light is a satisfying experience, even though the light was there before we entered the tunnel. We only realize the presence of light when we go through the darkness. Similarly, life is filled with peace and happiness, which we appreciate only after experiencing some conflict and sorrow.

Our first stop in Goa is the Madgaon railway station. First, we need to go to a lodge to unpack. We have a lodge in Fatorda for our stay today. For most of the journey, we will stay in dormitories and shared rooms because they are more affordable. Hope you remember the budget! :) Goa is full of beaches and has a rich Portuguese history. Normally, a tourist visiting Goa would go to a beach, swim in the sea, visit some heritage sites, and then enjoy some wine and food. So, will we do the same? Not exactly. We will try to see all aspects of Goa. There are shuttle bus services that connect different places within Goa, and they're electric too. So, we will use one to reach Panaji, the capital of Goa. The roadside view is filled with short trees, and we can't spot any buildings. Panaji is a small city but busy with tourists and shoppers.

Nothing is particularly interesting in Panaji until we head to Dona Paula via the Dayanand Bandodkar Marg, which runs alongside the Mandovi River. The river is filled not with water but with casinos and cruise boats. We won't find that many casinos anywhere else in India. The roadside is crowded with cloth vendors and fashion shoppers, creating a busy street market. Traveling through the inner streets also gives us insight into the Goan lifestyle, which is colorful and vibrant.

In Dona Paula, we get a good view of the bay and the unending Arabian Sea. Just stand here, feel the breeze, and enjoy the beauty of the sea waves. There are also three or four other beaches within a 1 km radius. Beaches, beaches everywhere! But no matter how many beaches Goa has to offer, we are not going to get into one just yet. Patience, mate. We will surely get to one somewhere else! :) The Dona Paula beach pavilion is not exactly a beach; it's a viewpoint. The area is filled with small vendors, and everyone seems to sell almost the same items. Some vendors actively attract customers, while others scroll on their phones. It would be better if the vendors offered different items so that the less salesy ones could also make some money instead of competing with others. See, our world is filled with competition, which is part of our survival instinct too. However, as we become more educated and informed, it's time for us to embrace an approach of cooperation rather than competition. Let synergy prevail! Let everyone win!

After Dona Paula, we are heading to Vasco Da Gama. Confused? Haha, it's a city named after the Portuguese explorer himself. The journey alongside the Zuari River is beautiful. We have plans for Vasco Da Gama, like visiting a fort and a Japanese garden, but we can't do anything. Guess why? Because there are no public transport options! We see everyone moving in private or rented vehicles only. Since it's about 10 kilometers to walk, we can't walk. The only thing we do in Vasco Da Gama is eat biryani. As colorful as Goa is, so is the food! The plate is filled with rice in red, blue, green, and yellow! It all tastes the same, though. We wait for more than half an hour to get our food, just like the cat that sits beside us. :)

Actually, nothing worked out for us in this place. Better to leave! We can try going to some beach at last, but again, bad luck. The shops, transportation, and attractions are all closed by around 7 pm. After returning to Fatorda and walking around disappointed for an hour, we survive on two apples from a street vendor, as there aren't any open restaurants nearby! Our evening in Goa is a disaster. But don't worry. This kind of situation happens very rarely throughout our journey, and it's okay. Sometimes, things won't work out the way we plan. We just need to cope with it, learn from our mistakes, and hope for a better tomorrow. Everything will be alright :)

Day 4

Run… run… run… When we have a train to catch and we're running late, this is what we tell ourselves—maybe a hundred times; who's counting? Due to the lack of public transport in the morning, we find ourselves in a race against time. A rickshaw driver shows his skills to help us reach the station. To get inside and find our train, we still need to run another 1-2 km. And remember, we're running with a rucksack on our back that weighs 10 kg! We need to move quickly while making sure the bag straps don't tear. Thanks to the rickshaw driver and our morning energy, we luckily manage to board the train just in time.

Today, we have one main destination: Hampi. As the train moves, we pass through the lush green hills of the Western Ghats. We get to see one of the best waterfalls in India—Dudhsagar Falls. It's spectacular. The water cascades down the mountain, looking like milk pouring from above. That's how white and beautiful it appears. The name "Dudhsagar," meaning "sea of milk," is aptly given. We can see it clearly from the train—not the milk, but the waterfall! :)

The journey from Goa to Hampi takes around 7 hours by train. We're in a sleeper coach, where the seats are long enough for us to sleep or for multiple people to sit. A young guy comes straight toward us, gives us a tough look, and sits next to us. We don't speak any of the languages he knows, and he doesn't speak ours. Since the seat is supposed to be shared, we accommodate him. However, he acts like he owns the entire seat! When the ticket examiner arrives, our seatmate quickly makes himself scarce. Guess what? He didn't have a valid ticket! We've been fooled! Realizing this, he apologetically collects his things and leaves. What a drama! Funny, though. This reminds us that all the drama others create will eventually come to an end. When we realize this, we can either laugh it off or dwell on it and seek revenge. The outcome is up to us. Let's choose to let go and enjoy the ride instead. :)

With such interesting experiences, we finally reach Hampi. As we enter the heart of Hampi, we start to believe the history lessons we learned in school. We realize that those lessons were not myths; seeing is believing! There are around 10 different historical sites and archaeological ruins scattered across the area. Since the distance between these sites is significant, walking would be quite difficult. The taxi and rickshaw drivers see this as an opportunity and are ready to take us on board! :) After some bargaining, we agree on a fare of 500 rupees for 2 hours. Finally, we're off to see the real gems of Hampi!

We visit many sites, including the Underground Shiva Temple, the Royal Palace, Lotus Mahal, Elephant Stables, Zenana Enclosure, Old Ponds, and bathing places. These 14th-century sites, combined with the big rocks scattered throughout Hampi, undoubtedly make it a UNESCO World Heritage site. At many sites, we take the time to imagine how people lived during those ancient periods. We can visualize the royal family residing in the palace, devotees praying in the underground temple, royal guests being hosted in the enclosures, and ordinary people bathing and washing clothes in stepped tanks—festivals being celebrated all around. We can even imagine ourselves as one of those ordinary people, maybe as a servant to someone else. This keeps us thinking about the transformations in civilization and society. Comparing today's century with those centuries, we realize how lucky we are in terms of freedom, ease of living, and equality. Instead of complaining and worrying, we should be more grateful for living in this era. Whenever we feel bad about the world and our lives, we just need to visualize ourselves as that ordinary person in ancient times. We'll come to appreciate what a world we're living in! What a life it is!

We also venture beyond the major attractions. We step outside the fort boundaries, view the sites from different perspectives, traverse less-traveled paths, and explore inner rooms and spaces. This gives us a clearer picture of the site, its history, its culture, and the lifestyles of ancient peoples. So, how do we find the time for all this? The answer is simple: "No photography." Throughout this journey, we won't capture any photos for ourselves. No pictures of us, the places we visit, or the people we meet. We also avoid news, phone calls, emails, and social media during the trip. Basically, we stay uninterrupted. These choices allow us to fully immerse ourselves in the journey and the experience. :)

Coming back to our exploration, that's all for Hampi. Since Hampi is in a very remote area, there isn't much to see nearby. So, we're heading somewhere else by train and bus—someplace far away…

Day 5

Today, it wasn't the circadian rhythm or the mobile alarm that woke us up; it was the bus conductor. In case you forgot, we were traveling by bus. When we travel at night, our means of transport also serve as our accommodation. So, when we reach our destination, the conductors ensure we wake up and get out. We're now at Shivaji Nagar, close to the center of Pune city. It's early morning, and since nothing is open at this hour, we look for a place we can enter. The Pataleshwar Cave Temple is the perfect spot. A peaceful 8th-century temple carved into rock. We are the only visitors in the temple compound at this time, accompanied only by a few pigeons. Enjoying solitude is a special feeling; the soul truly revels in such peace! Later, many devotees arrive to perform rituals, and only then do we realize it's an active temple. As the temple grows more crowded, it's time for us to escape. Oh, the pigeons managed to escape before we did! :)

Pune is an interesting city. There's a lot of energy, plenty to see, and much to explore. Unlike the past few days, today we will visit many places. After a short walk, we arrive at Shaniwar Wada, an ancient palace fort of the Peshwas. Almost everything inside the fort is accessible, with no hidden gems. From the top floor, we enjoy a stunning view of the garden. Great work, old landscape designer! The fort is located in the city center, so inside its walls, it's completely peaceful, while outside, the city bustles with activity. We notice that many visitors seem lonely, maybe seeking solace. When we don't have a person to comfort us, it's better to find a place that can comfort us. Shaniwar Wada is one such place.

As we stroll through the city, one place catches our attention: a museum named "Darshan." It's one of the most technologically advanced spiritual museums. Inside, we're taken through the life of Sadhu Vaswani, an educationalist and sage. With magnificent artistic sets, spatial experiences, holographic representations, and various technical applications, the museum beautifully combines spirituality with biography. Here, too, we are the only visitors at this time. Without hesitation, the guide takes us across the 10,000 sq. ft. interactive museum for a 1-2 hour tour. She is very respectful, even though she knows we have nothing to give back. However, we purchase a couple of books written by the sage himself. He advocates social service, frugality, vegetarianism, and more. Such ideas prompt us to reflect and question our everyday choices, possibly altering the course of our lives. To seek answers for a better life, we must start questioning, right? After all, how can we know how to live better if we don't examine our current way of life?

After taking a nap at our today's accommodation near Swargate, we head to the Pune-Okayama Friendship Garden, an elegant Japanese garden.

Here, we could peacefully walk around, enjoy the flowers, and spend hours gazing at the colorful fish in the ponds. It's so captivating that we never want to leave. Sorry, garden; we need to go! Since it's evening and everything is starting to close, there's nowhere else to visit. We'll simply transit across the city, maybe a bit far. So, we're heading to Pimpri Chinchwad via the rapid transport bus. It's a large industrial and highly populated suburban area, evident from the big brands, stylish buildings, busy roads, and faster transport systems.

As we move around Pune, we notice two uncommon things. The first is the bus stops. Normally, bus stops around the world are located at the side of the road, but in Pune, they are in the middle! In the center of the road, there are small raised platforms where we can board and disembark. We only get a few seconds to jump on or off the bus. It's so quick! While we read the destination sign and try to figure out where the bus is going, it may have already left the station. Sometimes we have to let go of the bus so that people in a hurry can board without incident. Don't worry. This experience can serve as a unique method for developing patience. :) The second uncommon observation is the use of scarves. We see that most girls and women cover their faces with scarves, especially those who drive. This isn't necessarily due to religious or cultural practices; it's more a fashion choice. It's interesting. It protects against pollution and heat while also enhancing privacy and confidence. It takes a while to figure that out. Some things take time; we just need to wait, just like we did for the right bus. :)

Day 6

As we mostly stay in dormitories and shared rooms, we get to chat with many people. Yesterday, a guy from Rajasthan in our dorm came to Pune to take an exam. As we shared the story and the journey so far, he became very excited. He expressed deep admiration and wished us the best. It's not just him; we receive such comments from many people throughout our journey. Their admiration makes us feel like we're onto something big. Who in this world doesn't want to leave their troubles to explore themselves and the world? Most likely, nobody. Yet, we often fail to prioritize such experiences over our relentless race to success.

Don't know if it was the excessive exploration we did or the overwhelming admiration we received, but today we're down with a fever. Oh yes, that's part of the journey too! But don't worry, we will travel and rest simultaneously. With that in mind, we're taking a bus journey to Mumbai. The 5-hour ride takes us through the smaller towns of Maharashtra and ends at the new-age urban city called Navi Mumbai. Note that Navi Mumbai and Mumbai are two distinct cities. When we are physically weak, nothing really matters; we won't even remember what we see. The places, the nature, the people—everything fades away. That's why it's better to seek new experiences when we feel physically well. Anyway, we need to get to our accommodation, which is near Dombivli, Thane. It's a place somewhat equidistant from Mumbai and Navi Mumbai. Since we're low on energy today, we can't take multiple buses or figure out the routes. Better hop on an auto rickshaw (aka *tuk-tuk*).

As we reach Navi Mumbai around 5 pm, what can we expect? Traffic! The city is buzzing. Auto rickshaw drivers are skilled enough to navigate the traffic and help us reach our destination faster, but only if there's enough fuel in the vehicle! As you can guess, the fuel runs out, and it's time to fill up. There's a long queue of more than 50 rickshaws lined up, and we must wait around an hour at the petrol station! Yes, one hour!

Since the driver wouldn't agree to cancel the ride, we have no option but to wait. :(

By evening, we arrive at our lodge in Dombivli. To add to our series of mishaps today, there's no one at the reception. We call, ring the bell, message, and do everything we can. After a while, the person finally shows up with a dramatic entrance—smoke filling the room, the scent of flowers, bells ringing, loud music playing, and orange lights all around. It's like the hero's entry in some old mythological television show. You might be wondering why. It's the daily evening *puja*! Chanting prayers and performing *arti* with *Om Jai Jagdish Hare* music playing in the background. He walks straight toward us in the small lobby but ignores us, fully engaged in the rituals. We can only watch the ceremony and wait for the room keys. Oh, dear lodge manager, you could have sent someone earlier so we could've escaped that smoke. Sorry, but we're sick today!

Day 7

Hoping that proper rest would reduce the fever and get us back on track, we take a couple of paracetamols and sleep deeply until noon. Only when we wake up do we realize that things have worsened. In addition to the fever, we now have diarrhea. Oh no, another day to pass without traveling. Don't worry. Just like race cars need a pit stop, it's time for a pit stop in our journey. If you remember, in the beginning, we discussed keeping an extra week for any contingencies. That is meant for days like today. A day to rest, recollect, rethink, replan, and refresh. Such pit stops are applicable throughout our lives. This long journey itself is a pit stop in life. Everyone has pit stops, though they come in different forms. Some take them knowingly, while others find themselves in these situations due to circumstances beyond their control. Vacations, holidays, career breaks, academic failures, breakups, financial difficulties, medical illnesses, family conflicts, and loss of loved ones are all various forms of pit stops. We can see them as opportunities to reinvent ourselves. Unlike race car pit stops, the pit stops in real life often need to be faced alone. Every time we find ourselves at a pit stop, we must push ourselves to emerge stronger. So, whatever problems we encounter, remember to take a pit stop and come out stronger. It's not the problems that matter; it's how we approach them that matters.

During our pit stop today, we also need to maintain a positive approach. We sleep for a long time, revisit our journey so far, plan the route for the next week or two, book the necessary train tickets, repack our rucksack, and hand-wash some "essential" clothes, all while coping with the fever and diarrhea. Thanks to online food delivery apps, we can order some diarrhea-friendly food too. Our medicine kit helps us manage our problems ourselves.

Ultimately, the entire day and night are spent within these four walls. Like everyone who faces problems and feels upset, we might consider quitting the journey and going back home. Going home sounds like the perfect solution, right? Not really. Remember, we are on a journey to explore India, ourselves, and the philosophy of life. No matter what, we will continue that journey. It's time to emerge from the pit stop, stronger!

Day 8

Even though our health isn't great, we're setting out for exploration today. Since central Mumbai is a bit far from Thane, where we're staying, we need to take a train to the city center. As we walk to the railway station, we can feel our energy levels dipping. Hmm, we need to eat something. The streets are bustling with various vendors, but surprisingly, there are no restaurants. After a few kilometers of walking, we finally spot a café. One notable aspect of the streets of Mumbai and its nearby regions is that people dine while standing. Yes, really! The cafés and restaurants often don't have chairs. We simply stand, eat, and leave. It's unclear whether this is due to a lack of space or because people are too rushed to sit and dine.

As we eat a couple of idlis while standing, we suddenly feel that something is off. Our eyes keep closing, our hands are fumbling, our legs are losing strength, and our mind fades away—until we finally collapse! Oh, no. Thankfully, a few nearby people lift us up, provide a chair, and sit us down. They even offer to take us to the hospital. Very kind! While people may not have time to sit and eat, they are more than willing to spend time helping those in need. Such moments restore our faith in humanity and reflect what we truly value. This alone makes us feel much better.

After resting for a while, we resume our walk. Don't be afraid. To ensure we don't fall again, we either lean on nearby objects or use handrails where available. Luckily, we reach the railway station safely. Mumbai's suburban railway system is fascinating. It's like a blend of metro and traditional trains, with fast-moving trains connecting major stops via conventional railway stations. The sights from Mumbai's railway stations and train journeys illustrate the city's overwhelming population density. However, it doesn't mean people ride on top of crowded trains as depicted in movies; that might have been the case years ago, but not anymore. Stations like Chhatrapati Shivaji Maharaj Terminus are beautifully developed, both inside and out.

Upon arriving in Mumbai's center, we walk to Horniman Circle Garden to take a much-needed rest. Given our current health, we require proper breaks along the way. The garden is filled with people enjoying their time in peace. Some read quietly, others nap on the grass, and some engage in deep discussions, while we sit worrying about our health. As we rest near a tree, we observe small rats scurrying about in search of food. We also ensure there's a washroom nearby, just in case our stomach calls. Remember, we had diarrhea yesterday.

Walking around the Bombay Stock Exchange and similar buildings evokes a serious feeling, since a lot happens in those buildings that make or break people's finances. Better to stay serious! :) Continuing our stroll, we reach one of Mumbai's most iconic landmarks, the Gateway of India. Set against the backdrop of the Arabian Sea, the monument appears majestic. The pigeons surrounding it and tourists posing for pictures enhance its beauty. The nearby Taj Palace Hotel stands as a testament to Mumbai's history and pride.

As we explore these attractions, we spot the Heritage Bus—a double-decker with an open roof that offers a city tour. We hop on board. The bus tour gives us a great feel for the city, showcasing the beauty of Marine Drive, the progress of societal development, and the variety of human lives. Mumbai is known for being home to hustlers, from billionaire businessmen to small business workers. We missed out on places like Dharavi and Dhobi Ghat, where the essence of Mumbai truly lies. Maybe next time.

We do manage to visit the Chhatrapati Shivaji Maharaj Vastu Sangrahalaya, a modern museum in Mumbai. The well-arranged museum, built in the Indo-Saracenic style, showcases history, art, culture, tradition, and science. It feels more like a carefully managed heritage site than just a museum, making it well worth the visit. However, the problem with museums is that we often don't remember much after leaving. They can provide knowledge and immediate excitement but rarely offer experiences that linger in our minds. Throughout our journey, we'll visit many museums, but only a few will leave lasting impressions. We'll see which ones those are and what experiences stick with us. Keep traveling!

Day 9

With all the good and bad memories, it's time to leave Mumbai. Our days here exemplify resilience. The challenges of our health issues, the place we stayed, and the warm weather made for difficult experiences. We could have simply packed our bags and gone home, but we showed the determination not to quit. Thank you for being part of those struggles!

After repacking our belongings with a refreshed mindset, we head to Bandra Terminus railway station. Adieu to the fascinating suburban railway system! However, it's a 3-4 km walk to the station from where we last were. This walk runs alongside the rails. As we stroll, we notice some construction workers' families living nearby, including very young working adults, their babies, and children. The sad reality is evident in the state of the children. They seem to lack access to hygiene, nutrition, and education. They look skinny, half-naked, barefoot, and unbathed. Yet, they're happily playing in the mud with paper boats. This scene strikes us deeply and lingers in our thoughts as we continue our journey. What does the future hold for these children? What are we doing to help them? How can they find joy in such circumstances? These are tough questions, and we'll seek answers as we move forward.

So, where to next? We're heading to Vadodara in Gujarat, also known as Baroda. Since it's already afternoon, we won't have time to explore much. But, as usual, the train journey is amazing. This time, though, the train is a bit different—more like a goods train, with many coaches filled with items for transportation. There are also many security personnel and their trained dogs. Don't know if there's a bomb on the train; let's hope not! :)

Train journeys are one of the best meditation techniques. When we gaze out of the window, countless thoughts arise, often unexpectedly. The very thoughts we've been seeking. Additionally, train journeys provide glimpses of the development, culture, and natural beauty of the places we pass. The interesting thing is that we gradually transition between locations, making it difficult to recognize the differences easily. This mirrors life itself; we gradually transition through ages, and it's not always apparent how we've changed as we grow older. Recognizing who we really are requires self-reflection. Ultimately, our consistent self-reflection leads to self-realization, a deep pursuit of knowing ourselves. By being mindful of our actions, words, and intentions, we can effectively navigate this journey. That's it!

As we near Baroda, it's late at night, and we'll have dinner on the train. Regardless of the location, our train food is always either roti-sabji or veg biryani. We can't afford to risk diarrhea again!

Day 10

Dormitory stays are special. Almost every guest wakes up early, gets on with their lives, and motivates late risers to get out of bed. We connect with people from different parts of the country and the world, each with different intentions. We also get a glimpse into the lives of others without breaking their privacy, which is increasingly challenging in today's privacy-conscious world. Our dormitory accommodation in Vadodara offers this social living experience.

When we talk about social living, it means a lot. We have to make compromises, trust others, keep mutual respect, and behave properly. For example, we might need to compromise on the AC temperature or the lights-out time. We must trust that others won't rob us and respect each other by keeping our voices low. Additionally, we need to avoid showcasing our awkward habits. Thus, staying in a dormitory can be considered a challenge that enhances our adaptability and confidence. On the positive side, it's been around ten days since we started our journey, and have you ever thought about how our clothes smell? They stink, seriously! But don't worry. Thankfully, the dormitories provide laundry service. They genuinely care about the needs of backpackers and solo travelers, offering exceptional experiences. Keep it up, good dormitories; you're very helpful!

Today, we will explore Vadodara, its history, and culture. The best place to start is the museum, so we're heading to the Baroda Museum and Picture Gallery. This old museum features collections of history, sculptures, artworks, zoological exhibits, and more. Museums serve as proof that history isn't a collection of lies. This museum proves that statement, not just for Baroda or India, but for other foreign places as well.

Surprisingly, we notice that we're the only solo travelers around. Couples and groups of friends are everywhere. It stirs the loneliness quietly resting within us. See, there's definitely a relationship gap inside each of us. It can be a gap between ourselves, our family, friends, spouses, partners, or society in general. Our goal should be to identify those gaps, determine their order of priority, and create an action plan to address them. This plan can also include simply waiting. Sometimes, that persistent waiting can make relationships truly marvelous.

Moving on, we head to a small town called Sevasi to experience life outside the city center. There's a stepwell here that is breathtakingly beautiful and showcases the splendor of ancient architecture, even though it remains largely unexplored by tourists. Apart from us, there's also a girl posing for some professional photography.

To our surprise, we stumble upon some festival celebrations—it's Ganesh Chaturthi today! A large rally is making its way through the town, as the local people of Sevasi gather to join in the festivities. More than a hundred people crowd the road, with loud music blasting from the processional vehicle, vibrant traditional dances performed by both men and women, and an endless shower of paper confetti flying through the air. What a spectacle! We join the dance rallies, blending into the festivities like locals. After hours of celebration, it's finally time to move on. We also need to stop by a phone service center. Having used countless different charging ports throughout our journey, our phone has become so confused—it's discharging very quickly. We need to fix it soon since it's essential for navigation and transportation. But don't worry; we won't get lost. Let's keep moving!

Day 11

When we're traveling and sightseeing, there's a constant urge to not miss anything worth visiting. Since we are in a city closest to the world's tallest statue, how can we not go see it? That would be a regretful oversight! So, we are heading to Kevadia, also known as Ekta Nagar, the site of the Statue of Unity and its surrounding attractions. It's a town rebuilt for tourism! As we travel from Vadodara to Ekta Nagar by train, we pass through various farming landscapes of rural Gujarat. From ground-level farming to hilltop agriculture, the journey helps us appreciate the scales and possibilities of farming in this region. The train is primarily for tourists, so there's a palpable enthusiasm among the passengers. Our seatmates are bombarding us with questions, assuming we're locals, and we respond as best as we can. In the end, they realize that we are also just like them. :)

Upon reaching the railway station, we find shuttle buses to the statue location. They know just where to pick us up. After passing through security checks, we can enjoy the beauty of the Narmada River and the impressive Patel statue while standing on a moving walkway. We ascend to the upper floors via escalators for a closer view of the statue. The scorching sun ensures we won't look up for too long! The true scale of the statue can only be appreciated when we're standing right next to it. But it's not just the statue; the museum and the surrounding area are remarkable. The information about the history and life of Sardar Vallabhbhai Patel, whom the statue depicts, is enlightening. Ekta Nagar offers so much more, including gardens, parks, and additional attractions, but we must move on.

While arriving in Ekta Nagar is easy, leaving when we want is not. Since it's a small town, public transportation options are limited. We hope to find a bus stand that Maps has indicated. However, upon reaching the location, we realize there isn't a bus stand at all. We are officially stranded! But it's okay; don't worry. With that big rucksack on our back, let's keep walking. Fortunately, a policeman comes by and offers us a ride to the railway station. What a relief!

So, when is the next train back? Around 7 pm. And what time is it now? 2 pm. So what are we going to do at the railway station? Reading! Yes, we can spend our time with the Sadhu Vaswani books we bought at that museum in Pune. Besides reading, we can take multiple naps on the train station seats and simply wander around. The station is completely free and peaceful—a great environment for meditation! As we sit here waiting for the train, we can start thinking about why things don't work out in life the way we plan.

It's easy to get frustrated about the wasted time. But maybe, instead of seeing this as wasted time, we can view it as an opportunity. Normally, when things don't work out, we get angry and want to quit everything. But don't quit; instead, change the approach. This principle applies to happiness and fulfillment as well. Some of us work hard to make money and buy happiness, some spend time with loved ones to experience happiness, some appreciate the beauty in everything, and some find happiness in what they do. There are countless paths to happiness. So, why are we so stubbornly sticking to that one path that we dislike? Do we really need to hold on to it? Let's leave it, get out of that trap, and find the path meant for us. While it may be a tough decision, it will be worth it in the long run. And if we've already found that path, let's reflect on it frequently because what feels right today may not necessarily feel right tomorrow. Life goes on…

Day 12

Today is going to be a busy day as we explore Ahmedabad, the largest city in Gujarat. With so much to offer and only one day to spend, there's no time to waste! As we get out of bed in the dormitory early this morning, we step outside into the vibrant hustle and bustle of the city. Street vendors and working professionals are already starting their busy days.

In the midst of this vibrant city lies a tranquil gem—the Sidi Sayed Mosque. This open heritage mosque features outstanding latticework and architecture, making it one of the best places for meditation. Inside, we witness silent rituals and prayers, with pigeons playing near the ablution pool, and we marvel at the beauty of the artistic works. We emerge feeling refreshed and energized. It's heartening to see that such historical monuments are still well-maintained.

Next, we visit Teen Darwaza, a grand historic stone gateway adorned with three beautiful arches, located in the middle of a busy market. Our love for art and architecture leads us to the Hutheesing Jain Temple, a historic temple boasting stunning carvings. We could easily spend an entire day simply appreciating the intricate details of the craftsmanship. Our respect for the ancient artists who created these works deepens as we witness the rituals and activities inside the temple. The magnificence of the temple itself fills us with positive energy.

Ahmedabad's beauty lies not only in its architecture but also in its rich history, nature, and development, all centered around the Sabarmati River. Mahatma Gandhi's Sabarmati Ashram and Museum transports us back in time, outlining the principles, thoughts, and life of Gandhi. The peaceful atmosphere of the ashram encourages deep reflection on what we've seen and learned in the museum. We sit on the veranda of Gandhi's room, watching someone use a spinning wheel, mindful of his legacy. We purchase some of his books to read on our journey. What's interesting about Gandhi is how he combined spirituality with practicality to inspire societal change. His actions have motivated millions, making him one of the greatest leaders the world has ever seen!

As we move on to witness the beauty of nature and modern development, the Riverfront is a perfect destination. The vast and artistic flower park invites leisurely strolls, and the Atal Foot Over Bridge, with its captivating light show, adds to the excitement. The modern infrastructure surrounding us is impressive, complementing the serene flow of the Sabarmati River.

Oh, there's one more place we visit in between. Don't want to lose the Sabarmati flow; hence, the revisit. :) We also stop by the Shree Swaminarayan Museum, a peaceful modern complex that displays and explains the life of the revered yogi, Swaminarayan. In the middle of our explorations, we pause for some delicious samosas and tea. With so many sites to visit, we don't follow a strict meal schedule today; we simply eat whenever we get the chance.

For dinner, we enjoy a proper vegetarian biryani at a nearly empty restaurant. The workers are engrossed in a cricket match on TV, and even the waiter, while serving our food, kept one eye on the game. His enthusiasm was contagious, tempting us to watch along with him!

While sports can build unity and teamwork, they can also foster a mindset that equates winning with defeating others. This mentality often seeps into other areas of life, where success is viewed as outdoing others instead of self-improvement. True success is not about defeating others but about becoming a better version of ourselves.

Day 13

Before we leave Ahmedabad, it's important to mention the people we met in the dorm—young individuals from different parts of the country. Some had been staying in the dorm for months, working remotely and building their own businesses! We had a great time sharing our life journeys and experiences. Our collaborative attempts to fix a broken air conditioner were also quite enjoyable. It's always the challenging situations that transform a group of strangers into a team, creating lasting memories.

With those memories in mind, we are moving on. As it's raining, there's a good chance things are going to get messy today. From the Gita Mandir bus stand, we're taking a public bus to Udaipur. Yes, we're leaving Gujarat for Rajasthan, the largest Indian state by area. Since it's raining heavily, the bus windows are shut. All we can do now is read or reflect. By afternoon, after a 6-hour bus journey, we arrive in Udaipur. The city offers wonderful attractions like beautiful lakes, palaces, museums, gardens, and parks. But nature isn't on our side today. The city is flooded, roads are closed, and everything is shut down.

We manage to get an auto rickshaw ride to the Udaipur Palace. However, in the middle of the ride, a huge stream of water begins flowing through the streets. As the water level rises and starts entering the vehicle, we have to turn back. We ask the driver to move forward as much as possible, but since it's his vehicle, he can't afford to take that risk for our sake. So, back to the bus stand!

Since there's not much we can do at this moment and to avoid getting stuck in the city for long, it's time for us to leave. We've set foot in Udaipur, and that's about all we can manage today. From the same bus stand, we're off to Jodhpur now. The panic is palpable across the city. People rush for transportation, shouting and speaking loudly. The sad faces say it all. No matter how grand our plans are, sometimes nature has other plans. But that's okay. We just have to accept it and move on.

We can approach such adversities positively by considering the much worse scenarios that could have occurred. For example, if we had been stranded in those flooded areas for too long, we might have lost all means of transportation, faced the risk of drowning, or encountered an electric leak in the water that could have been fatal! This doesn't mean we should dismiss the situation entirely. Instead, we should be thankful for having avoided these extremely unfortunate possibilities. This mindset can transform a negative situation into a more positive experience.

As we get closer to Jodhpur, nature appears more peaceful. At least now we can open the windows and see the world! Surprisingly, the bus takes us through village roads, even though other highways could have made the journey faster. This route allows us to glimpse the culture and lifestyle of Rajasthan's villages: small grocery stores everywhere, groups of people socializing under streetlights, cattle sheds attached to houses, and the beauty of Rajasthani attire. It's worth taking those less-traveled roads, even if they were unintentional and unexpected. We should believe that every unfortunate situation can lead to something positive. We just need to have faith and look for it.

Anyway, that's enough positivity for today. It's late at night, and we will rest now. We have a bunk bed waiting for us in a backpacker's hostel.

Day 14

While it rained heavily yesterday, today we're greeted by a scorching sun. Just to remind you, we're currently in Jodhpur, the blue city of India, located near the Thar Desert. What else can we expect but this heat? :) But it's much better than getting stuck in flooded areas. Comparison changes the way we see things, doesn't it?

Jodhpur is known for the Mehrangarh Fort, the city's key landmark, and that's where we're heading first. The fort has been transformed into a museum, and it's very well maintained. Walking through the steep corridors of the fort transports us back in time. Scenes from our favorite historical epic movies run through our minds. Along the way, traditional musicians provide the perfect instrumental music, creating a captivating backdrop. While everyone is busy taking pictures, we choose to sit with those musicians, enjoying and appreciating their art. The more interested we are, the more energized they become. That's what all artists seek—to receive appreciation for their craft, which inspires them to give their best. Let that be a reminder for us whenever we meet an artist!

As we ascend the fort, we're taken through various palaces, where the rooms, artworks, and historic collections are a feast for our eyes. To top it off, the terrace offers a picturesque view of Jodhpur, revealing thousands of tightly packed, blue-painted houses and buildings. If you had any doubts about why Jodhpur is called the Blue City, hope it's clear now! :)

At the top of the hill, it's time to descend. We are going to take the road less traveled—a narrow path that winds through the blue-shaded buildings and wall paintings. It's blue everywhere! The narrow path also provides an insider's view of homes in Jodhpur. Speaking of home, sometimes it's not the easiest place to return to. There's a deadline for the trip, but here we are—still far away. What now? A solution is needed, right? So, we're heading to a quiet spot in this bustling city to think deeply about how to handle the situation. This quiet place is a walkway near Gulab Sagar, a large and deep man-made heritage lake used as a reservoir for the city's domestic needs.

As we sit there contemplating, a man suddenly rushes in on a bike, abandons it on the road, and jumps into the lake! Suicide attempt! He begins to drown and starts screaming. In an instant, a few neighbors come with a rope, throw it to him, and attempt to rescue him. But he's reluctant to be saved. Then, a brave man jumps into the lake, rope in hand, grabs the drowning man, and ultimately rescues him. Fortunately, he survives. The scene unfolds in less than a minute. The man emerges from the lake crying, while his mother confronts him, and some people try to console both of them. The quiet place quickly becomes crowded. After a few minutes, everyone disperses, returning to their routines, and we sit there processing what we just witnessed.

Just wondering how big his problems might have been that it led him to suicide. Suicide is not a solution to anything, but it reflects the intensity of the problems. Now we realize how small our problems are compared to that man's struggles. Often, we overthink our issues, overestimate their impact, and over-hurt ourselves. We should strive to simplify our lives in every aspect. Simplification can lead to fewer worries. A huge salute to those brave souls who volunteered to save a life! Sometimes, we just need someone like them to pull us up from the depths. But who will pull us up when there's no one but ourselves?

Near Gulab Sagar, there's also a historic step well. Thankfully, there isn't enough water to drown anyone here! As we walk through the city, we find a clock tower and its associated market. It's a central landmark surrounded by local shops and vendors. The streets are bustling with people, vehicles, and cows all mixed together. It's fun to watch!

After all the unique experiences Jodhpur has offered, we're now leaving for Jaisalmer, eager for new experiences and learnings.

Day 15

Our stays are always limited to low-cost accommodations, but those experiences are memorable. Our hotel in Jaisalmer had a cultural ambiance and offered great views of the fort and the city, even though the room lacked proper lighting and locks. We sleep with the hope that we'll wake up alive and well. But don't be afraid. Even in a luxury hotel, we can't be entirely sure we'll wake up the next day, right? So, it doesn't really matter. What matters is our inner strength and the practical precautions we take. We still have that pepper spray in our pocket!

As we step out into the city in the morning, we can truly feel the desert: sandy roads, heavy winds, extreme temperatures, sweating, and thirst—it's exhausting! Hats off to all those who live in these arid regions. And to the camels, too!

Jaisalmer lies in the heart of the Thar Desert. So, what are we going to do? Camel safari? Jeep safari? Desert camping? Sorry to disappoint you, but we're just going to roam around. Near the city center is Gadisar Lake, an attractive artificial lake. The decorative architecture surrounding the lake, the peaceful atmosphere near the temple, the hundreds of catfish by the lakefront steps, and people feeding bread to them—all these sights make us want to linger forever. The golden reflections of the morning sun enhance the lake's beauty. With the sandstone architecture and the desert sand, the entire Jaisalmer has a golden hue.

The Jaisalmer Fort is also within our sight, tempting us to visit. But we have other plans. We're taking a local bus to Thaiyat, where a war museum is located. Due to the low population density, public transportation is limited. As we wait like the locals, the bus becomes overcrowded with goods, vegetables, luggage, and, of course, passengers. Just so you know, we're the only outsiders on that bus. The same is the case for most of our bus trips. It's okay, no problem.

Then what's the problem? The bus stops 5 km away from the war museum. There are no people, no vehicles, no livelihoods—nothing in sight. We could try hitchhiking, but no vehicles are going in any direction. Basically, we're now stranded in the desert! We also can't rest on the road for long because there's no shade. So, with a 10 kg rucksack on our back, under the scorching sun, we are going to walk! There's a good chance we might get dizzy and pass out along the way. But don't worry, that won't happen!

After walking for about 1-2 km, our savior appears: an army officer on his motorbike. Just seeing another human is a huge relief! Thankfully, he gives us a ride to the museum. The war museum is very informative, showcasing military history and an impressive arsenal. But the journey was more memorable—and challenging, in fact. As the saying goes, the journey is more important than the destination. That applies to life as well. The steps we take to reach our goals shape who we are as individuals, and that's more important than simply achieving the goals, isn't it?

Now we're heading back to Jaisalmer city. Hunger is calling. Our go-to food choices in these northwestern regions are either roti with mixed veg curry or a complete veg thali meal. We are not going to experiment much with food because we can't afford extra days of diarrhea!

We have a train to Jaipur this evening, and we still have some time to spare, so let's take a walk. Right in the city center is a small building called the Desert Cultural Centre—a museum showcasing the culture of Rajasthan. Interestingly, they also run a puppetry show, and luckily, we arrive just in time. Although we got tickets, it feels a bit skeptical since there's no one else around to watch! We wait for about half an hour, but unfortunately, no one else shows up. Still, the organizers are ready to proceed.

It's a live puppet show performed by a puppeteer along with two other artists. It turns out to be one of the best live artistic performances ever, and they did the show just for us! Pure goosebumps! Immense appreciation for the commitment of those artists and the people who run the show. This kind of hidden gem deserves more visibility and support from everyone. There are thousands of such great artists and art forms unnoticed in different parts of the world. Let's make sure we uplift them as much as we can.

Day 16

Jodhpur is blue, Jaisalmer is gold, and Jaipur is pink. It's like each city in Rajasthan has its own theme, which is evident everywhere—from the railway stations to buildings, markets, and places of attraction. And now, we find ourselves in Jaipur. On our way to Hawa Mahal, we observe the city's operations. The way the shops in the markets are structured is commendable; each shop is identical in terms of architecture and is numbered sequentially. So, if you want to find a shop in the Jaipur market, just look for the shop number. No need to remember the name, address, or landmarks. It's brilliant! When everything becomes numbered, life gets simpler and more interesting, doesn't it? The progress we make toward our goals, the miles we travel, the calories we burn, the money we earn or lose—give everything a number, and life becomes more interesting!

Hawa Mahal is a simple yet beautiful palace, mainly because of the geometric design and the surrounding ambiance. It's worth a look from the outside. Outside, hundreds of street vendors sell juices, hats, ornaments, clothes, toys, gadgets, and more. It's fascinating to watch people bargain, with some engaging in negotiations with no intention to buy, just for the sake of it. After observing this a few times, we can almost feel the vendors' frustration. It's a perspective we don't often see, is it?

Near Hawa Mahal is the City Palace. Maybe because we've seen so many grand palaces already, it doesn't capture our attention anymore. It's time to explore something different, something more natural. What better choice than Smriti Van, an urban forest and biodiversity park? We're going to take a long stroll along the park trail, which promises to be interesting since we'll be surrounded by small wild animals and plenty of peacocks. We can't take our eyes off the captivating dance show that the peacocks put on. Experiencing that in the solitude of a forest, with the peacocks just a few meters away, gives us pure goosebumps! It tempts us to stay there forever. We must admit, there's nothing more amazing than the beauty of nature. No art, technology, luxury, or relationships can compare. Nature is unbeatable. Sadly, Smriti Van closes by evening, so we must leave.

Temples are good places to visit when everything else is closed, and Akshardham Temple is nearby. The architecture is impressive, with a well-maintained leafy garden and clean surroundings. We might not see such perfection in many temples—or maybe we just haven't visited enough. Anyway, we will visit more temples, mosques, churches, and other places along the way to experience different cultures, rituals, perceptions, and beliefs.

Speaking of culture, it's also reflected in our accommodations. Today's dormitory is a bit different from others; it's artistic, adorned with vibrant wall paintings. Surprisingly, we're supposed to sleep on the floor, but good mattresses are provided. Normally, every stay offers a bed and cot, not just a mattress. We can either embrace this positively and sleep peacefully or take a negative stance and create a fuss. You know which attitude we're going to choose!

Day 17

Get up! We have a morning train to catch. Today, we're heading to Agra, known for its iconic representation of Indian tourism—the Taj Mahal, one of the Seven Wonders of the World. So excited! With the village views along the way, we arrive in Agra by afternoon. Luckily, we find a cheap hostel within walking distance of the Taj Mahal. No time to waste now; let's walk toward the wonder!

The path to the monument is well-structured, and as we move forward, we sense we're about to experience something extraordinary. The tight security checks only heighten that anticipation. After passing through a few gates, there it is—the white epitome of love! An architectural marvel indeed. To enter the mausoleum and see the tomb, we need an extra pass. While many visitors don't take that extra step, we can't skip it. We're meant to explore the inside, aren't we? Of what stands before us, and of what lies within us. :)

Inside, it's quiet and empty. With no one around, we softly sing a few lines of our own music, and it echoes within the walls. Goosebumps! We've imprinted our music on the Taj Mahal's marbles and tomb. By the way, those marbles are really huge and beautiful. Outside, we also get to see the beauty of the Yamuna River flowing quietly.

From that peaceful atmosphere, we transition to the bustling city, where the roadside is filled with small vendors selling snacks. Agra Fort is the main attraction near the city center. An ancient red sandstone fort with large courtyards, gardens, and palaces inside. It's spacious, and the buildings inspire us to envision royal events, processions, and historical moments. We spend some time resting and daydreaming before stepping outside.

As we exit the fort, we're approached by small children asking for food and money as charity. This poses a tough dilemma. If we help them, are we fostering dependence on charity, which may not be beneficial for their future? Conversely, if we choose not to help, are we contributing to their starvation or illness? There's no straightforward answer here; it's a complex situation. We are going to try something different—let's learn about their lives. We take a few children to a nearby vendor and buy them food and juice. We all eat together and share what we have from the same plate. They seem disinterested in conversation, but after a few attempts, they start to open up about their lives.

They live in the city slums, don't go to school, rely on charity for survival, and have parents who do the same. Surprisingly, they all express happiness in their lives. This leads us to talk with the vendor. He has a degree, tried various jobs, and now runs a street food stall in his thirties. He introduces us to the concept of "Free Life," which he describes as a lifestyle choice of some people. A life where everything is provided for them, freeing them from worries. He explains that while there are free schools and programs to help children attend school and parents find jobs, many families neglect those opportunities because they are content with their "free life."

So, why do we feel the need to "fix" the lives of people who seem happier than us? Why impose our views and beliefs on those who have no interest in changing? Why care for those who didn't ask us to care? It's a complicated question.

Among the many children we meet, one named Rohan stands out. He's around ten years old and wants to go to school to become a soldier. Unfortunately, his parents are uninterested in sending him to school as it doesn't provide immediate benefits. Currently, he sells used bottles and scraps to help support his family. That's his life. Rohan's dreams are trapped by his challenging family circumstances. And there are probably many other children like him who are deprived of the chance to achieve their dreams, simply due to the situations into which they were born. It's not their fault; it's the harsh reality of their ancestral chains. We can choose to ignore them, help them survive, or give them the wings to fly. The choice is ours.

Day 18

There's a popular misconception that traveling is always thrilling. What do you think? It's not always the case. Sometimes, it's exhausting, and we just don't feel like waking up and going out, especially when there's no one waiting for us unless we risk missing checkout time! Anyway, it's time to leave Agra and head to New Delhi, the capital of India. The bus is full, and a fellow passenger shows interest in our journey. Our conversations delve deep into relationships, responsibilities, the purpose of life, and much more.

A common thread emerges in these discussions: everyone dreams of traveling like we are, but many feel held back for various reasons—lack of time, confidence, funds, or awareness. It's all about prioritizing and making compromises. Everything in life is just like that: what we prioritize gets done. Anyway, for us, each compliment we receive is fuel for our onward journey. Proud of you for being part of this adventure so far!

Delhi is incredible! Well-organized areas, massive apartment complexes, extensive metro, bus networks, modern infrastructure, and easy access to everything, all while preserving its diversity and heritage. Plus, it's the second-largest city in the world by population! A lot of planning has gone into building and maintaining this city, and we can only hope that pollution levels improve in the coming years.

Our accommodation in Delhi is in a bustling market called Main Bazar in Paharganj. This area is vibrant, with hundreds of shops, restaurants, and accommodations crammed into a small space. The narrow roads are alive with people, auto rickshaws, bikes, cycle carts, street food stalls, and even cows. Everything is so lively that we'll bump into a vehicle, a cow, or another person if we close our eyes for just a second! The railway station and metro stations are just a short walk away, adding to the lively atmosphere.

A one-kilometer walk through the lively streets leads us to our hostel, where we find ourselves in a room shared by ten others—definitely a budget stay! But that's fine; all we need is a safe, cheap place to keep our stuff and lie down at night.

As evening falls, what do we do when everything else is closed? Yes, visit a shrine! We're heading to Nizamuddin Dargah, the shrine of the revered Sufi saint, Nizamuddin Auliya. There's a song called *Kun Faya Kun* from the Hindi movie *Rockstar*. It portrays the hero's journey—from being expelled from home to hitting rock bottom and seeking hope and refuge at this very Dargah. It's deeply emotional and very relatable. And now, we are here to experience it!

As we enter through a narrow passage lined with vendors selling flowers, scarves, and religious materials, we politely decline their offers. However, we soon realize we're the only ones without headscarves inside the shrine! But our timing is perfect, as the evening *Qawwali* music session is underway. A lead male singer with a harmonium, accompanied by a small group of musicians, sits near the tomb floor, offering melodious devotional songs. We stand here, absorbed in the music, then gradually sit down, move closer to the musicians, and finally become part of the supporting musicians! Singing and clapping along to songs we hear for the first time, without even knowing the lyrics or meaning. It feels magical, just like it was for the *Rockstar* hero.

After the music session, we notice many people rushing somewhere. It's *langar* time! The Dargah provides free food to those in need, including many homeless individuals. We queue up alongside them, waiting patiently. Although plates or containers are required to collect food, we only have a small plastic cover from our first aid kit. With no other option, we accept the Dal curry in it, along with two rotis. Sitting beside the Dargah walls, we share the meal with others from the queue. They have no one to care for them, nothing to survive on, and nowhere to go but the Dargah. This moment serves as a powerful reminder that we are all just flesh and blood. Where is the ego? Where is the social status? Where are the possessions? In the end, nothing really matters.

Day 19

Delhi is immense! There's so much to see, explore, and experience, and we will try to tackle it all, one by one. Our first stop today is Qutub Minar, a stunning minaret that showcases the architectural brilliance of the past. The height of the minaret makes us tilt our heads back in awe, but the morning sun ensures we can't hold that position for long. The lower stories of the minaret are enough for us to appreciate its grandeur. Being alone gives us the luxury of time; we can indulge in whatever we want. This doesn't mean we're off duty, though. We get tasked with helping couples capture their perfect photos, and that too with the entire tower in the frame! :) Still, we can do things others might restrict themselves from, like lying on the grass under a shady tree, playing with squirrels like children, and soaking in the beauty of the minaret all at once. We can call this either mindfulness, laziness, or maybe a mental disorder. How we label it reflects how we see the world.

As the sun moves away from our shady spot and the squirrels bid farewell, it's time to leave. How about we go somewhere different and modern? A premium place where corporate professionals work, socialize, and unwind. Welcome to Cyber City in Gurgaon! Since we arrive after noon, the atmosphere is calm yet lively. Small groups of well-dressed individuals in business attire share jokes and laughter, either heading to or returning from upscale eateries. Those who are alone are typically wearing headphones talking to someone or listening to music. In the midst of all this, we find an open space where we can sit on the steps. Oddly enough, we seem to be the only ones just sitting here.

What do we do? People-watching, of course. We observe the hundreds of faces passing by, taking note of their emotions and trying to discern their states of mind. Some appear genuinely happy, while others wrestle with insecurities, and some seem to be desperately trying to fit in. If you were in one of their shoes, which role would you play? Or would you rather not be here at all? Why?

As you ponder that, let's catch a rapid metro back to Delhi. Unlike the underground metro within the city, the Gurgaon to Delhi metro is elevated, offering us a bird's-eye view of the surroundings. Underground is boring, all we see is darkness. Every place is the same, just dark :) Anyway, before it gets too dark, we need to visit the Red Fort. As the largest monument in Delhi, it's celebrated for its architectural splendor and historic significance. Inside the fort is expansive, featuring large audience halls and beautiful gardens, reminiscent of the Agra Fort we visited. However, this fort has seen much change—different rulers, rebellions, attacks, demolitions, and more. Lucky for it, it still stands strong. As evening sets in, the lights cast a captivating glow over the fort, enhancing its allure. Just as we begin to take it all in, security personnel remind us that it's closing time.

There's still one more stop we can make—India Gate. It shouldn't be closed since there is nothing to close as such. But wait—entry is restricted! A major inauguration is happening tomorrow, with heightened security in place. No worries! Thanks to public transportation being available late at night, we can continue exploring the city for as long as we like. Until the sleep calls :)

Day 20

Delhi is home to two significant institutions: Parliament and Supreme Court. These are places where people look for hope and where change happens at scale, impacting 1.4 billion lives. Tremendous, isn't it? Imagine merging such institutions across countries to create a centralized law and governance system. Envision a world where everyone follows the same laws, has equal opportunities and resources, and experiences a sense of unity. No inequality, no wars, more cooperation. Quietly, we are moving toward this, one step at a time. A new world is coming!

Unfortunately, we couldn't get inside either of those institutions today due to tight security restrictions for the inauguration ceremony. We'll find out more about it this evening. For now, let's seek some peace. What could be more peaceful than a museum dedicated to a man who advocated for peace his entire life? We're heading to the Gandhi Smriti Museum. This museum showcases Gandhi's life, the struggles he endured, and the values he upheld. Before it became a museum, this place was his residence, and it's here that he was martyred. The calmness permeates the entire compound. When we leave, we're filled with peace, motivation, and a broader understanding of morality. It's a divine atmosphere!

A similar essence can be found at the Lotus Temple, though it's a bit farther away. The Baha'i House of Worship is a religious site open to people of all faiths. This modern, magnificent structure is designed for meditation, although that purpose may be a challenge to fulfill during peak tourist hours. Nonetheless, its architecture is stunning and rivals Delhi's historical architectural brilliance. Hats off to the creators!

As evening sets in, we have one significant task left: discovering what's happening in central Delhi. It turns out to be the inauguration of a ceremonial boulevard named Kartavya Path and a statue of Subhash Chandra Bose, a prominent Indian nationalist. This is a major event, not just for Delhi but for the entire country. The Prime Minister, numerous ministers, and many dignitaries are attending, which explains the heightened security measures. We can see thousands of police officers and their vehicles mobilizing across the city. It feels like there are more police than civilians here!

We remain hopeful that we can still be part of the event, but no, there are barricades everywhere. Oh, it's an invite-only event! We try to get in through various entry points, but luck is not on our side. Better to obey the rules than risk getting arrested! So, what now? We'll wait on a nearby road until the event concludes. We have some company too: a few media personnel, a handful of young locals, and plenty of police officers. PM Modi's speech echoes nearby, and experiencing such an event from the outside feels to be more fascinating than being inside. Why? Because we get to observe various dignitaries arriving, the security convoys, and the behind-the-scenes work that makes everything run smoothly.

Usually, who cares about what happens offstage when the focus is on what's happening onstage? Who pays attention to those unsung heroes who ensure everything works well behind the scenes? Who remembers the important people that have helped us shine in our lives? We can!

By the way, the event is over, and we can finally get inside. We're among the first civilians to witness the new statue and the newly inaugurated boulevard. Media representatives are still filming videos, and some attendees are continuing to roam around. Standing here, we also see India Gate shining with tricolor lights. It's a grand feeling overall, and we're lucky to be part of this event, as uninvited guests :)

Day 21

After three days of intense exploration and fascinating experiences, it's time to leave Delhi. Typically, we spend a maximum of one or two days in a city, so three days in Delhi feels like a record—congratulations! Undeniably, Delhi is vast, and we definitely needed those three days as a bare minimum. A few things worth mentioning are the cleanliness of the main roads, the affordability and taste of the street food, and the organized numbering system for public transportation. Small details matter and create lasting impressions.

From the New Delhi Railway Station, we're heading to Chandigarh. As it's morning, we get to witness the inner parts of Delhi during the train journey. The most striking scene is the apartment complexes: hundreds of old, fully occupied buildings densely packed together, with washed clothes hanging on many window bars. The roads are narrow and filled with private vehicles, presenting a stark contrast to the Delhi we just explored. Now we see clearly where the millions of people in Delhi live.

The scene changes dramatically as we arrive in Chandigarh. It's a planned city designed from the ground up by an architect. That's exactly why we're here—to explore what makes it different. A glance at the map reveals that Chandigarh is a large rectangular grid, featuring numerous symmetrical squares in between known as sectors. The sides of those squares are the roads, the vertices form the road junctions, and the areas within are designated for residential and commercial purposes. Fascinating, huh?

Before we dive into the city center to explore its geometric architecture and residential layout, we need to secure accommodation. As we discussed before, we typically book our stays online, hoping that the listings are genuine. This time, however, we're in for a surprise. As we search for our accommodation, we wander into a residential area, finding ourselves between homes. Sensing that something is off, the locals join us to help. After thorough exploration, we discover that the lodge doesn't even exist! When we contact the online booking company, we find out that the listing is fake. Agh, what a waste of time for everyone involved!

Dealing with this incident consumes our afternoon. At least we still have the evening ahead. As usual, everything is closed, and we head to a popular garden nearby only to find there's no light or electricity due to renovations. What a lucky day, huh? But are we going to let that settle us down? Absolutely not! We are going to get a bike taxi and explore the city instead. Remember the rectangle and square grids? Yes, we'll navigate through the sides of all those squares. Luckily, we get a young rider who starts showing us around his hometown like a guide. He takes us through the industrial, residential, and commercial areas. The roads form the lines in the grid, and we encounter a traffic signal (stoplight) every 1-2 minutes—something the rider isn't too fond of either! Despite that, he promotes his city like it's the best place to live on Earth, not just because of its geometric structure, but because of how the city functions. It's built with modernization and urbanization at its core.

However, a one-size-fits-all approach may not always work because we're all built differently, right? Yes, we're constructed uniquely from the ground up. :) How we build ourselves ultimately determines who we are, why we're here, and where we're going. Build wisely!

Day 22

The only reason we came to Chandigarh was to see and experience what's different. Have we achieved that? Hmm, to some extent, but not fully. It's okay; we're not journeying to research places. Our primary goal is to explore ourselves and the philosophy of life as we traverse India. We have no time to waste! Let's go. There is a train to Amritsar.

What about breakfast? Just because we're boarding a train early in the morning doesn't mean we'll starve until we arrive. There are plenty of options: we can buy packed food upfront, purchase cooked breakfast from vendors at the stations along the way, or even order food online to be delivered at the next stop. If all else fails, there's usually some passenger nearby eager to share their food. Our breakfast choices mainly consist of idli, samosas, biscuits, and sandwiches. The point is, we'll never starve on the train! The same goes for Amritsar. No one goes hungry here thanks to the community-run free food service called *langar*, offered at the Golden Temple gurudwara. Right after we arrive in Amritsar, that's our first stop.

Entering the gurdwara is a special experience. We remove our shoes, put on a yellow headscarf, wash our feet, and only then can we enter the gurdwara. This process instills a sense of holiness, almost as if we're washing away something. The next level of this experience is taking a holy dip in the pool. Inside the gurdwara feels like stepping into another world. A majestic temple made of marble and plated with hundreds of kilos of pure gold. We've arrived at just the right time; the gold glistens brightly in the afternoon sun!

To protect the temple and serve visitors, we see hundreds of volunteers and security personnel dressed in traditional Sikh attire, wielding swords, knives, and spears. Intriguing! The soulful background music enhances the divine atmosphere. We stroll around the pool, observing and soaking in the beauty of this small world. *Langar* is particularly fascinating. Driven by countless volunteers, this community kitchen provides free meals to anyone in need throughout the day. As we enter the hall, a long queue awaits the next round of serving. We join the line, wait our turn, and receive plates and glasses before sitting on the floor. Volunteers serve us a variety of food items, all of which taste very good. But we must eat quickly since each round accommodates around a hundred people and lasts only 10-15 minutes. It's perfectly organized, serving thousands of people daily—absolutely commendable! We could stay here forever, but we need to move on.

All major attractions in Amritsar are located in the city center, and the crowds reflect that. Just a few steps from the temple, we arrive at Jallianwala Bagh, a garden and memorial dedicated to the massacre that occurred in 1919, claiming hundreds of protesters' lives. The associated museum recounts this tragic history. The sorrow is palpable in the eyes of every visitor. It's a mix of regret and respect. A feeling that makes us all feel guilty for the sufferings and losses of others. It's so painful. We need to put an end to all forms of misuse of power, from acts like this to large-scale wars. Transform greed into generosity, superiority into equality, and hate into love. Then only we will be at peace, inside and out.

As we exit the garden, we find lots of taxi drivers waiting for us. Where to? Why now? What for? It's for the flag-lowering ceremony at the Attari-Wagah border, which will be happening soon. At the India-Pakistan border, security forces from both countries conduct a ceremonial function every day and allow the public to participate. These shared taxis will take us there. What are we waiting for? Let's jump in!

After about half an hour, packed into a single auto rickshaw with ten others, we arrive at the border alive! Even though we didn't pre-book anything, we get a balcony view in the stadium. The patriotic music, dance-like movements of the soldiers, and the crowd's cheers create an electrifying atmosphere. This is where patriotism peaks. We can see that while half of it is genuine, the other half is simply peer pressure. Regardless, our taxi driver is waiting for us to return. Remember, if we delay, nine other passengers will also be delayed. Let's not do that.

As we head back to Amritsar, we return to the Golden Temple to experience its evening ambiance and, of course, to take part in the *langar*, again! :)

Day 23

Not everything in our journey is planned. Sometimes, it's about going with the flow. Today is one of those days. All we know is that we're heading to Kashmir, but we don't know how. This marks the beginning of our exploration toward The Himalayas mountain range. Very excited! That excitement motivates us to catch the 5:30 am bus to Jammu. Yes, we're taking a bus that early because we have no idea what lies ahead.

Reaching Jammu feels like a dream, especially since we've been sleeping most of the way. We're dropped off somewhere in Jammu, but we can't check our location on our phones. Why? Because our normal SIM and internet don't work here. Without internet access and maps, we feel like lost birds. So, our first goal is to get a working SIM. The nearby shopkeepers are quick to capitalize on our situation, treating us like royalty and selling SIM cards like precious jewelry. It makes sense; for us, access to the internet is now the most valuable thing. We often don't realize the value of something until we lose it, right? Consider time, memories, health, relationships, family, etc. As we age, we will inevitably lose them one by one. It's a hard truth. Are we valuing them enough today?

With our new SIM, we figure out that we're near Jammu city center. Our destination is Srinagar, Kashmir. Unfortunately, there are no buses available right now. By the way, don't expect any train journeys for a week—it's the Himalayas, after all! Our only option is a shared taxi. We pile into a taxi with five strangers, and it will take us about ten hours to reach Srinagar. Just a heads up—Srinagar is known for frequent terrorist attacks! What do you think? Go or no go? You can join if you don't want to get stranded. :)

Inside the taxi, we're joined by two construction workers and a couple planning to visit their family. We try our best to communicate, but language is a barrier. More importantly, we're too busy enjoying the breathtaking beauty of nature. The majestic mountains, narrow valleys, and rivers flowing deep below are absolutely scenic. We're glued to the car window for the entire journey! Nature is so stunning that we can't take our eyes off it. To top it all off, it starts to rain. Goosebumps, again!

As we approach Srinagar, we begin to see security forces everywhere. They check our bags and belongings to ensure we're not going to cause any trouble. Jokes aside, in the city center, it gets serious. We see gun trucks, checkpoints, barricades, and lots of military personnel at every road junction. Arriving at night, we witness strict patrolling throughout the area. It feels like we're in a war zone. Immense respect for the people who live here every day!

Everything closes early, so our only task is to find accommodation and sleep. We have a booking for a lodge, but when we arrive, they inform us it's full. Agh! It's late at night, and there aren't any affordable hotels nearby. We're in trouble. But don't worry. Who's there for us in times of trouble? The soldiers. One soldier arranges an auto rickshaw for us to take us to a place to stay. He leads us to an interesting option: Dal Lake. Wait, we asked for accommodation, right? Yes, we're staying in a houseboat on Dal Lake. No worries, it's common here. Many people stay in houseboats and floating hotels anchored along the sides of the lake.

We're taken to our houseboat in a small wooden boat called a Shikara. The houseboat is constructed entirely of wood, featuring a small room with a wooden cot—but no door lock. A simple dinner and free TV entertainment come complimentary. As we settle in, we're left with a lot of uncertainties, the safety of the houseboat, the security of our belongings, and our own safety. The chances of getting robbed, drowned, or worse feel very real tonight!

As you know, not everything is planned. Sometimes, we just need to go with the flow. It may lead us to the right place or the wrong place; we'll never know. Face the odds—that's life.

Day 24

Luckily, we're alive! We didn't get robbed, we didn't drown, and we didn't get attacked by anyone. Our stay in the houseboat was much more peaceful than we expected. :)

Time to go. Saying goodbye to our houseboat hosts is a bit emotional—not because we'll miss them, but because of the bargaining involved! It was a bit pricey, but that's okay. The free Shikara rides compensated for it because the morning beauty of Dal Lake is breathtaking! The serene water, the reflections of sunlight, and the view of hundreds of houseboats are simply stunning. However, as we hit the roads, the sight of gun trucks wipes away those feelings. Our minds shift back to thoughts of safety and security. Safety first, mate, safety first. We also need to find safer and cheaper accommodation today, so that's our priority before we dive into more exploration.

One main issue we face in these mountainous areas is the lack of public transportation services. It's not easy to find a bus or taxi, so we're going to do a lot of walking. So is everyone else. It's also interesting because we get to cross the majestic Jhelum River on various bridges. Rivers are what make the Kashmir mountain valleys magnificent. The significance of the Chenab and Jhelum rivers deserves a mention.

As we walk into the city center, we aim to find a hotel. Guess what? We run into booking issues again! Srinagar, you're giving us a lot of trouble with accommodation—it's unacceptable. But we're not giving up this time. We even find ourselves in a position where we help the hotel manager review the online booking console and fix the issues. And we get it sorted! As a token of appreciation, the manager drops us off at the nearest bus stand in his car! Is that a good thing or a bad thing? After all, we're trusting a stranger for a private ride. Anyway, we did it. By the way, have you ever had a negative experience with trust? Has someone you trusted ever disappointed you? How do you feel about that now? Just think about it. See, trust is a game. We take our best shots based on others' words and actions. Many times we win, and sometimes we lose. But the more we play, the more we learn about the game—the game of trust. So, keep playing! :)

From the city center, we catch a bus to the taxi center. From there, we need to get a shared taxi to Tangmarg. Then, we'll need another shared taxi to reach our destination, Gulmarg, the meadow of flowers. Yes, a lot of transfers! But as we get accustomed to the shared taxi system, it becomes more interesting. It feels like we're being part of helping people with their commutes, even though the driver is collecting money. We accommodate as many passengers as possible, even though it can get uncomfortable sometimes. But the beauty of nature helps ease that discomfort.

As we travel the Tangmarg-Gulmarg route, the scenery becomes more captivating. There are lots of hairpin bends, sharp curves, and steep inclines. The mountainside is filled with small, beautiful flowers all along the way. As we reach Gulmarg, we're greeted by lush green meadows. It's green now, but in winter, it will be blanketed in white snow! There are plenty of activities to do here—horse rides, cable car rides (gondolas), ATV rides, paragliding, golf, and skiing in winter. Sorry to disappoint you, but we're not going to do any of that. Instead, we'll head into the woods and climb up the meadows without following any trails and all alone. All we have for company is a hen that has been following us for quite some time. There's no one else in sight.

We climb as far as we can, navigating hidden mud pits and steep inclines. Then we yell at the mountains—for no reason at all. Crazy, huh? When we go beyond boundaries, life gets crazier. Consider love, passion, spiritualism, materialism, and even media. When we exceed limits and cross boundaries, it drives us to extremes we never imagined. Before we reach that stage, let's descend the mountains and head back to Srinagar. That will be enough for today. :)

Day 25

If you remember, we started from almost the southern side of India, so reaching the northern side is a significant achievement. Today, we're making that happen with our journey to Leh, Ladakh. Congratulations on making it this far! Challenging times lie ahead, but you'll keep up our spirit. Yes, you will—you always have! That's why we're catching a bus at 7 am. Fortunately, there's a direct bus to Leh! We'll be traveling for 10 hours, covering around 400 km through the mighty mountains, with no access to food or shops in between. Let's pack some apples before we leave.

We have a high-class bus for our trip today, complete with large, viewer-friendly window panes, air conditioning, and a music system! Since it's going to be a long journey, it would be nice to make some acquaintances. We have three other guys on the bus of our age. All the passengers are here solely for the Kashmir-Ladakh trip, usually for less than a week. We're the only exception, as always. :)

As we move to the outskirts of Srinagar, we see wooden houses surrounded by apple orchards and a peaceful atmosphere that's completely different from the city center. As we drive further away from Srinagar, the intensity of that peacefulness increases. It reaches a level where we can't see any more houses, trees, or people. All we see are mighty mountains dominating the horizon. The red, brown, and gray mountains are beyond our imagination. The Sind and Indus rivers dance energetically, their silver waters flowing strong and swift. This entire view is breathtaking! The rugged mountain passes add to the thrill. At times, the passes are so narrow that part of the bus's wheels go off the road, facing deep valleys that would spell disaster for us. We see many trucks that have fallen into those valleys along the way!

Meanwhile, our driver seems to be creating his own adventures, taking shortcuts like crossing streams on the bus. Interesting, huh? There's even a moment when dust fills the air, and he stands up from the driver's seat to close the opposite window, all while the bus is moving at an average speed along the mountain pass! What confidence! Or is it reckless driving? Confidence is certainly a valuable quality, but overconfidence? Not really. No matter how good our intentions are, actions that could harm others will backfire one day.

Not everyone is heading to Leh; some passengers drop off along the way to explore other attractive places like Sonamarg. While we see only barren land and mountains, there are still people living in smaller towns. The population is very low—maybe close to a thousand. One foreign couple mistakenly takes someone else's luggage while dropping off, and the victim turns out to be one of the three guys mentioned earlier!

By evening, we finally reach Leh. We begin to see more people and can finally eat something, all while keeping the mountains in our sight. Our stay in a dormitory in the mountains ensures that connection.

Day 26

We endured a cold night in Leh, one of the coldest cities in India. Even more impressively, we braved a cold shower this morning—wow, good job! Cold showers often instill a sense of confidence, making us feel our bodies can survive anything. We'll see about that. :)

One fascinating feature throughout Leh is the Tibetan prayer flags. Mantras and prayers are printed on colorful clothes and strung everywhere, creating a beautiful sight. Just seeing those flags every day serves their intended purpose: promoting positivity across the region. Sometimes, having a positive intention can yield significant results, especially regarding mental and physical health. Maybe this is why Tibetan culture is so highly regarded for fostering a peaceful life. Anyway, we're going to explore more aspects of Tibetan culture, starting with the Leh market. As it's early morning, the market is nearly empty, with vendors just beginning to set up their stalls. We see many women arranging fruits and vegetables, knitting scarves, selling clothes and various other items. We'll check on their progress when we return in the evening.

As we stroll through the market, we encounter an entry gate leading to something unexpected. Upon entering, we discover it's a Buddhist temple and monastery, the Gompa Soma. This spacious, peaceful space is situated right beside the market. The golden-colored statues and decorations are a feast for our eyes, and the tranquility and positivity enveloping the temple nourish our minds. Buddha's love for meditation resonates throughout the space. It's hard to tell if people come here to meditate, pray, or do both simultaneously. The ultimate aim of spirituality is to know ourselves deeply, right? Wish it would happen to everyone.

Time to move on—maybe take a step back in time. We visit the Central Asian Museum, a well-maintained, small, yet insightful place showcasing the history of Central Asian trade. The displayed artifacts transport us back to the age of the Silk Route! What's even more interesting is the view outside: a bird's-eye view of hundreds of buildings, houses, shops, and the Leh Palace in the distance, all framed by the majestic mountains. We can sit here forever, gazing at that view. However, the sight of Leh Palace compels us to go there. It's perched at a high altitude, and we're uncertain if we'll make it. As we walk toward the palace and climb up the mountain, the trek becomes increasingly difficult. We might be the only ones in the city without winter clothes—we're surviving in a raincoat! Our breathing becomes labored, our bodies shiver, and our hands feel almost frozen. The confidence we built up from that morning cold shower is now shattered. What's the use of confidence if we ignore safety measures? We should have brought warmer clothing, but carrying that weight for the rest of our journey was not feasible. Remember the 10 kg rucksack? Yes, it's still with us. :)

After a disappointing attempt to reach the top of Leh Palace, we try something similar next. Thiksey is about a half-hour ride from Leh. Although there are shared taxi options, they aren't frequent. We go with the flow, find a few transfers, and finally arrive at Thiksey Monastery after about an hour. There's hardly anyone on the roads, but we're going to walk this time. The steep climbs on the road and the steps are tiring, but with multiple breaks along the way, we make it to the top! Yes, we made it—congratulations! :) The view from the summit is stunning. The barren land, the Indus River, and the distant mountains combine to showcase the beauty of Thiksey and Ladakh. While the Buddhist monastery contains small temples and accommodation for monks, it lacks the peace we found in the market temple, likely due to the influx of tourists. Ironic, isn't it? Most of the time, what we seek is right within our reach; we just need to look closely. :)

It's getting late, and we need to return before we get stranded without transportation. The Leh market in the evening is a completely different scene from the morning. It's now bustling with local vendors, buyers, and many more tourists. The woman who was knitting in the morning has now crafted a multitude of scarves. She's still knitting. Great work! The vegetable seller's baskets show little progress, likely due to the increase in vendors. As we wander through the transformed night market, two small girls approach us. They're both in early childhood, engaged in selling key chains and ornaments. We talk to them to understand their lives better. The older girl seems well-trained in handling this situation, evident from the series of lies she spins about her background. While the younger one tries to speak the truth, the older one swiftly changes the subject, pulling her away. Ah, the poverty trap! It's so disheartening. We worry for their future, and that concern fuels our hope that one day we'll work toward resolving such issues. Let's get back to the present and wind up for today.

Day 27

Today marks another full day of bus travel through the Himalayan mountains as we leave Leh in Ladakh for Manali in Himachal Pradesh. Catching the bus means we have to wake up at 4 am! As we walk toward the bus station in the early morning, the weather isn't our only challenge—it's the street dogs. Tens of street dogs bark in groups, ready to attack us. We would have been in big trouble, but luckily, a stranger offers us a ride in his car.

This bus trip is different from our touristy ride to Leh. We have an ordinary, affordable bus. The bus is packed with local commuters and luggage, leaving little room to walk between seats. We can barely sit comfortably, and this will be our situation for the entire day. Oh, everything comes with a compromise, right? Our entire life journey depends on the compromises we make. Each life decision is essentially a compromise—whether it's time, money, health, relationships, peace, freedom, or happiness. There are no major decisions in life that don't involve compromising at least one of these factors. Understanding what to compromise can significantly change how we approach decision-making.

16 hours—that's how long it will take us to reach Manali. Around 14 hours to Keylong, and then 2 hours to Manali. Sometimes, this journey spans two days with an overnight stay, but we're lucky that today's service will complete it in one day! The Leh-Keylong highway is

breathtaking, with twisted mountain passes, mighty peaks, and snow-filled regions. There are no houses, vehicles, or people—just the vast landscape, and also no network! This isolation makes the trip fascinating. The open-window bus allows us to feel the true environment—the air, the smells, and the weather. However, it comes with a heavy downside: breathing issues. As the bus ascends to higher altitudes, the oxygen levels drop, making it increasingly difficult to breathe. We really feel this at places like Taglang La, which sits at over 17,000 feet and was once the world's second-highest motorable pass. Fortunately, the bus stops here, and even though it isn't winter, the area is covered with a thin layer of snow. We get to touch it! Snow feels truly magical. :)

So far, so good—we're still breathing! However, as we continue our journey at these high altitudes, everything becomes increasingly blurred. Our mind, body, and stomach feel unstable. All we see are mountains, and now we can hardly comprehend their beauty. Surviving on apples and biscuits isn't helping either. When the bus stops at a food stall, we can only throw up! Throwing up in the mountains is a unique experience though. The heavy winds carry the vomit far away before it lands. The shortness of breath and lack of water make cleaning up also difficult. Overall, we feel like we're dying. What a fascinating journey, huh? The snow is no longer magical, and the mountains are no longer beautiful; we just want this trip to end. But we can't drop off in the middle—there's nowhere to rest and no one to help us. Don't worry; we'll stay calm and hope for the best. Enduring such situations alone helps us grow. The more we train ourselves to endure hardships, the better we mold ourselves as individuals. Words can't teach resilience; only experiences can. Embrace challenges, build up resilience!

Reaching Keylong alive is a relief. The next leg from Keylong to Manali will be quicker, thanks to the Atal Tunnel—a 9 km modern tunnel, the highest highway single-tube tunnel above 10,000 feet in the world. It reduces travel time by about 5 hours, making it very efficient! We arrive in Manali before nightfall. The market is still active, filled with vendors and tourists. From our hotel balcony, we have a bird's-eye view of the market and city center. The bustle of the city lifts our spirits for tomorrow's exploration, but for now, it's time to recharge. :)

Day 28

The first thing we do today is step out onto the balcony. We won't get balcony views every day, so let's make the most of it. And it's worth it! Hundreds of coniferous trees, the morning sun, and a calm market greet us. It's a stark contrast to what we saw last night. It feels like we've woken up in a different place. As it should be; that's what Manali is. A resort town meant to mesmerize visitors with its natural beauty and adventurous offerings. The perfect honeymoon destination. So, what are we doing here alone? We're also on a honeymoon—with our new selves. :)

Anyway, it's time to explore nature. Solang Valley is the best place for that. A half-hour bus ride from Manali takes us to Solang, where a plethora of adventurous activities awaits, making it a bit overwhelming to choose. Paragliding, ziplining, rafting, ropeway rides, ATV adventures—the list is endless. In winter, activities like skiing and tube slides join the lineup, all of which cater perfectly to newlyweds. In our case, however, our partner—our new self—prefers a quieter and more private place. That's why we'll take a walk along the peaceful road, away from the touristy spots. The green conifer trees enhance the mountains' beauty, and the Beas River beckons us. But how do we get closer to the river? There isn't a proper path to the riverbank. It's time to take some risks!

We are going to encroach on the grounds of a government construction headquarters. Instead of security restrictions, our challenge turns out to be the street dogs. Tens of them, silently approaching us step by step. We can't walk forward or backward; we're surrounded by dogs ready to strike. We're in big trouble. Don't worry. Just as we prepare to defend ourselves, a resident emerges and swiftly controls the dogs. Thanks to him, we're safe now. He returns to his home without even asking anything. Since we've come this far, let's walk down a bit more to reach the riverbank.

The effort pays off. The Beas River flows magnificently, hitting the rocks and forming grayish water in a cool atmosphere. Blue Whistling Thrush birds hop across the boulders, and the unending river is framed by stunning green mountains. Moreover, there are no humans in sight. It's just us and nature—pure goosebumps! Dipping our feet in the flowing river and sitting atop large boulders, we could linger here forever, simply enjoying nature. We feel a sense of happiness that we've never experienced before. Something truly magical! Wait, is this transcendence? Hmm, maybe. But it's subjective, anyway.

See, we never had any actual plan to sit by this riverbank in search of happiness; it was entirely unintentional. We simply went with the flow, and overcoming the obstacles along the way has added to our satisfaction. That's when we realize that unintentional happiness often influences us more positively than intentional happiness. The more we try to create happiness, the less we enjoy it. Remember when we were children? We didn't have many intentions, right? Life took us where it wanted, and we were happy. We were fully present in those moments, not worrying about anything else. Somehow, as we grew older, we began to idealize happiness in terms of so-called success and goals, altering our thought processes. We started chasing happiness and missed out on those genuine moments. So, are we living for the future or the present?

As we relax beside the Beas River, contemplating happiness, hours slip away. We don't want to leave, but we have to. As a souvenir from this incredible experience, we take three small, beautiful stones from the riverbank. That's the only souvenir we have from our entire trip across India! It's time to head back. On our way down, we face another challenge—a long snake lying in the center of our path. We try to encourage it to move with stones, tree trunks, and everything else in sight. Luckily, it eventually slithers away after a few attempts. The street dogs are gone too. Let's get out of here!

Even though we make it to the main road safe and sound, here comes another catch: there's no bus to return to town. Uh oh. No worries; we can explore the mountain flora while we wait! We stroll, checking out the various plants, flowers, and trees until the bus finally arrives. Back in Manali, we take a quick visit to the Hadimba Devi Temple, a 15th-century pagoda-style temple made of wood nestled in a deodar cedar forest. The path to the temple is like a small trek, but the architecture and religious rituals make it worthwhile. As evening sets in, visibility decreases, and fog begins to roll in. Before we risk getting stranded in the forest, let's head back down.

The Manali Bazaar is still bustling, filled with vendors, photographers, locals, and, of course, honeymoon couples. Watching these couples pose for photos always brings a smile to our faces. Hope you enjoyed our honeymoon in Manali. It was a bit different, purposefully. :)

Day 29

Today is an all-day travel day. By the way, we are halfway through our trip. Congratulations on being part of the journey so far; you're doing great! It's so lucky to have you along. We've spent the past 1-2 weeks in northern India, and now it's time to leave here for our next stop, Shimla.

We catch a morning bus and are fortunate to have a talkative co-passenger. It's not often we encounter such friendly travelers in the north, but this guy starts chatting as if we're old friends. He's a postgraduate student heading to college far from home. Our conversation flows easily, covering topics like culture, movies, lifestyle, work, travel, and, of course, some philosophy. He shares some apples and expresses the belief that owning and managing an apple orchard is the most respected job in the state. That's surprising because there is a common belief that being a government leader carries the most respect due to its scale of impact. For example, if a president or prime minister decides that the minimum wage needs to be increased, it would significantly improve the lives of millions of people! That's a substantial impact, right? However, now we realize that equating impact with respect is misguided. For society to function effectively, it requires the efforts of all of us, in different ways, whether through jobs or services. Each of our roles contributes to the larger ecosystem. It means all our lives and work are equally important and deserve respect, regardless of the money, fame, or power they may offer.

As we travel toward Shimla, we see more people, households, and human activity—something that had been lacking for the past few days. The vibe improves as we reach the heart of Shimla, where the markets, bus stands, cafes, and hotels lead us to The Ridge. It's a beautiful paved promenade that offers a stunning view of Shimla, accompanied by chilly winds. The Ridge is bustling with tourists, vendors, and locals alike. It seems perpetually crowded. The architecture, culture, and overall atmosphere feel strikingly different from what we've experienced so far; it's as if we've landed in another country! Well, technically, we didn't land; we just walked. :)

We could wander around here for hours until it's time for our next bus. Yes, towards Dehradun in Uttarakhand. It's going to be a long journey. Before we embark, we need to recharge ourselves and our phone. So, we roam around The Ridge, searching for a restaurant with charging points and affordable food. An interesting combination, right? But it's already evening, and we can charge our phone once we reach our accommodation, right? There's just one problem: we have no accommodation tonight! We'll be sleeping on the bus—just sit and sleep. It will be tiring, but that's okay. See, we need to experience everything: the good, the bad, and the neutral. That's the journey of life. The better we adapt to these experiences, the better we thrive. Happiness and peace don't come from our circumstances; they come from our ability to adapt to them. No excuses! :)

Day 30

It's early morning, and we've just alighted from the bus in Dehradun, only to board another bus to Rishikesh. So, yes, our actual destination for today is Rishikesh. You thought it was Dehradun, didn't you? :) Rishikesh is a Hindu pilgrimage city situated on the banks of the prominent Ganges River. It's a place of sages and yoga. It feels exciting to be here, but our "sit and sleep" approach on the bus has left us quite tired.

We check in at today's hostel, but there are no vacant beds until noon. So, we are going to take a stroll beside the Ganges. Luckily, we find some benches near Ganga Beach. Here we are, sleeping on public benches alongside a few homeless men. Let's enjoy this unique experience; after all, we don't get to sleep beside a river every day! As we rest, we begin to appreciate the beauty of the Ganges. It flows swiftly yet calmly, framed by lush green trees. People are bathing and practicing yoga on the beach. It's all so scenic and relaxing. Naturally, this leads us into a deep nap. :)

Afternoon naps are really good. A 15-minute nap can do wonders! You might want to give it a try if it's new to you. Anyway, we feel recharged now. After unpacking at our stay, it's time to explore. The Ganges is beautiful, but the view from Ram Jhula, the suspension bridge, reveals the river's mightiness. It's so wide and full of water, flowing with pride. No wonder it holds such significance in geology, history, culture, and the livelihoods of millions.

What's more interesting are the Ghats. There are tens, if not hundreds, of Ghats alongside the Ganges. Ghats are the series of steps that lead down to the river, often named for easier identification. They are always lively with pilgrims, rituals, and vendors. Sitting in a Ghat and doing nothing can be one of the most satisfying experiences. :)

One of our primary goals in Rishikesh is to visit an Ashram. To see what happens inside, how it works, and possibly find some spiritual inspiration. We walk along the Ghats searching for ashrams. Some are closed, some look intimidating, and some are just not genuine. But finally, we find the perfect match we're looking for—Parmarth Niketan.

It's a peaceful ashram offering yoga and meditation and is involved in various humanitarian activities. Plus, our timing is perfect; it's Ganga Arti time!

On the Ghat near the ashram, during sunset, the priests and residents perform the sacred *arti* ritual. The Ghat is now crowded with hundreds of devotees. The chanting of mantras, the offering of flowers to the river, the waving of lit traditional oil lamps, and the glow of the fire lamps, along with the devotional hymns and songs, all make the *arti* what it is. Spiritual, harmonious, and fascinating. Goosebumps!

Right after the *arti*, we attend a Satsang, a spiritual Q&A session with Sadhvi Bhagawati Saraswati, a major spiritual leader in the Ashram. She addresses a couple of questions and shares her thoughts. Interestingly, the session is in English, and the majority of the attendees are foreigners! By the way, we have so many questions that need answers, right? However, we can't be present here for this Satsang every day, so we need a solution. We obtain the contact email from an organizer and start sending a few queries each day. He passes them on to the superiors, and Sadhviji answers them during the Satsang, which we can watch live-streamed daily! They say our questions are great and encourage us to keep sending. :) Innovative, huh? But more importantly, insightful! This practice continues for many days, and the ideas enlighten us on various aspects of life. After all, it's often a combination and derivation of others' thoughts that shape our own thoughts, isn't it?

Day 31

We're in a spiritual mode now. Our journey has recently turned into a pilgrimage. No wonder Uttarakhand is called Devbhoomi, the Land of Gods! The Ganges, the sages, and the sacred places all awaken the spirituality within us. It feels like a transformation. Anyway, now, it's time to navigate to our next stop: Haridwar. It's just a one-hour bus ride from Rishikesh. Goodbye, Rishikesh! :)

Haridwar is quite similar to Rishikesh. Temples, ashrams, sages, and of course, the mighty Ganges River. Everything feels familiar. Oh, and the cooler weather we experienced in the Himalayas is gone; we're back to the heat. It slows us down a bit, but we must not stop. That grit motivates us to keep exploring. This leads us to places like the Shish Mahal Ram Mandir, a mirror palace and temple adorned with countless statues and idols, all reflecting beautifully. The artistic detailing of these sculptures, along with the 360-degree reflections, is fantastic. Reflections add to the beauty, don't they? Whether in water, sound or even a mirror, it holds true in most cases. Life is similar; self-reflection and how we reflect ourselves to others both showcase our elegance and enhance our beauty.

At the Bharat Mata Temple, we see similar sculptures and idols, but it's very different from a typical temple. The building resembles an apartment complex with its seven-story vertical structure. It honors freedom fighters and popular figures, functioning more as a museum, along with some deities and acts of worship. An interesting combination, right? That's why the temple attracts many tourists. In contrast, ashrams like Saptrishi Ashram are extremely quiet. Here, we can walk around and witness activities like cleaning, prayer, inventory management, education sessions, and more. Amidst all this, we can even hear the sound of leaves falling from the tree we're sitting under. Such is the silence in the ashram.

Silence is a skill to be developed, not a gap to be filled. Appreciate silence, and peace will be ours!

Not all ashrams share the same ambiance, though. Shantikunj Gayatri Parivar is entirely different. It's filled with loud devotional music, crowded guests, and lively chatter. As we venture deeper into the ashram, we realize it's like a complete town. The roads, residential buildings, schools, shops, auditoriums, museums, gardens, farming, water harvesting systems, and other facilities in the ashram reflect this. What interests us most is the free food, served as a religious offering rather than a mere dinner. There's also an acupressure walkway lined with medicinal plants on both sides. Walking along this path is relaxing, tickling, and a bit painful—all at the same time. But it's fun in a special way! :)

As we exit the ashram, we get back to the ordinary world. Walking alongside the road, we spot a small street food stall managed by a very young adult couple. It's a tiny shop with a couple of chairs, no specific kitchen, and everything covered with sheets! There aren't any other customers. And safety? Don't even think about it. What draws us to that shop is the couple. They treat us with the utmost respect. We may not receive such genuine care at any luxurious restaurant. Their cooperation, dedication, empathy, and love for each other are unparalleled. Hope this remains throughout their lives, and wish that their lives serve as inspiration to many. Where there is empathy, there is love; where there is love, there is paradise. Lucky us, we're in paradise tonight! :)

Day 32

After a couple of weeks of relying solely on buses, we're back on the train! Missed the train experience :) Our 10-hour journey takes us to Lucknow, the capital city of Uttar Pradesh. Yes, our accommodation for yesterday was the train, and we are now leaving Uttarakhand. Lucknow is a city with a population in the millions, modern infrastructure, and a rich heritage and history. We'll see what it has to offer, but first, the rituals: unpacking and refreshing ourselves. We've got a dormitory for that—one bed out of ten in a small hall. That's enough for us, considering the budget :)

Almost every popular city across India has a zoo, and Lucknow is no exception. Here, we visit the Nawab Wajid Ali Shah Zoological Garden, a zoo that was established over a century ago! Didn't know the concept of a zoo existed that long ago. It's curious how animals and birds were caged while people were fighting for freedom at that time. See, we've all visited a zoo, aquarium, or similar place at some point in our lives, and it's enchantingly beautiful. This Lucknow Zoo is no different; it houses many species that are managed and treated very well. Observing these different species allows us to appreciate the beauty of nature and find happiness. But what about them? Shouldn't they also experience freedom? Who are we to deny their freedom? Imagine being imprisoned for a lifetime without having done anything wrong. That's the reality for the animals in the zoo.

Within the zoo, there's also a state museum exhibiting ancient artifacts, sculptures, and mummies. Now we're getting into the history part, which we will explore further. Our next stop is the Bara Imambara, a Muslim shrine built in the 18th century by the early rulers known as Nawabs. It's stunningly grand, featuring a large garden in front, beautiful arches, an extremely tall ceiling, spacious chambers, antique lighting, and a complex maze leading to the terrace. The maze or labyrinth (whatever it is) that leads to the terrace is the most exciting part. Seems like there are a hundred combinational paths. We easily get trapped until we start following someone who knows the way. It's initially thrilling, then worrying, and finally a bit terrifying! From the terrace, we enjoy a wide view of the city and can sit here for hours. If the body allows, we can even sit inside the small arched windows visible from the terrace. :)

Now, we're in the heritage part of Lucknow. As we step outside the Bara Imambara, there's more waiting for us: an iconic watchtower, a monumental arch gate, a historic clock tower, a picture gallery, and much more. Each of these constructions features a unique style, with a focus on arches that enhance their beauty. Now we need to see what's happening on the ground. It's mostly leisure; the area is spacious, and we spot many adults playing serious cricket right beside these monuments. We can spend time meditating on the steps of an ancient human-made pond beside the clock tower, sipping some hot chai that's brought to us! There are tea vendors with kettles who make sure we drink at least one cup before we leave. The walkway beside Rumi Darwaza, the majestic arch gate, is lined with street food vendors selling savory snacks known as chaat. Those vendors also ensure we eat something before we depart. Cricket, chai, and chaat—three things that are common and beloved all across India! And we get to experience all three together this evening here in Lucknow. Hope you're enjoying it! :)

Day 33

Most of the time, our co-passengers on the train are families, especially during long-distance journeys. But today is an exception. On our morning train to Varanasi, our entire coach is filled with a group of multi-level marketers! Yes, around 50 people selling products through person-to-person sales. They booked the whole coach for their return journey from a training session in Lucknow. By chance, we ended up in between them because one member canceled his booking, leaving us with that vacant seat. As the journey progresses, we notice that most of their discussions revolve around schemes and "get rich quick" dreams! Each conversation reinforces their existing beliefs. It's an echo chamber—a silent threat to modern society.

This echo chamber phenomenon occurs in our everyday lives through our involvement in social media, news media, community groups, religious groups, political groups, peer groups, and even academic circles. We tend to see and hear more of what we already believe, and we are wired for it. How can we know our beliefs are right or wrong if we don't even consider the reasoning behind other beliefs? Essentially, we all exist in an echo chamber. But when we break free from it, a new world opens up. A world of fresh ideas, varying perspectives, and possibly truth. This shift allows us to think and act differently. Our beliefs will change, our character will change, and we will change.

Anyway, back to our co-passengers. They start introducing us to their team, company, products, and schemes. From groceries to stationery to electronics, they have everything to sell. By the time we reach Varanasi in the afternoon, we know almost everything about their system. What else can we expect when we're trapped with an MLM team? :)

Varanasi, also known as Banaras and Kashi, is historically and culturally significant. Considered the oldest continually inhabited city in India, it's famous for its Ghats and is a central destination for Hindu pilgrims. And to add to that, the Ganges River flows here. It's come a long way, hasn't it? :) As we approach the Ghats, the city is bustling. The roads and streets are filled with vehicles, tourists, pilgrims, and vendors. What's more interesting is the narrow corridors leading to the Ghats. We walk along these small paths, flanked by residences and shops, which connect to many similar pathways. Our accommodation is also somewhere in this maze. After a lot of wrong turns and backtracking, we finally arrive at the Varanasi Ghats.

One of our goals in Kashi is to visit the Kashi Vishwanath Temple, a famous Hindu temple. With numerous entry gates, security restrictions, and modern amenities, it feels quite different. We've visited many temples, but this one seems very people-centric. Once we pass through the gates, we see the queue to enter the temple. After waiting for around half an hour, we reach the inner gate. Guess what? One more queue. It's a gate within a gate within a gate! :) It takes about two hours to pass through that final gate. Getting out of the queue once you're in is not easy either, so it's best to just let it be. Inside the queue, we find ourselves tightly packed in a large hall. We observe some people quietly praying and meditating, others patiently waiting to give their offerings, some chanting mantras loudly and energetically, while some are networking, and others impatiently eager for their darshan. We even notice a few fainting in the queue! All are devotees and pilgrims, mostly elders. Their willingness to make sacrifices is commendable. The degree of devotion to someone or something can be measured by the sacrifices we are willing to make for them. This applies to both non-living and living entities, including deities, humans, relationships, work, interests, ideas, principles, and even material possessions. Anyway, the wait is finally over—we're inside! The interior is elegant, and we get a few precious seconds for the darshan before we can peacefully roam around the temple. No more queues! :) Now we see happy faces, relieved after the wait. For many here, visiting this temple is a lifelong dream, and we can see that fulfillment reflected in their expressions. What we seek, we achieve. What we achieve, we cherish.

The queues in the temple take longer than we expect, but now we can walk around and explore more Ghats. Close by is the Manikarnika Ghat, a large area for cremations right beside the Ganges. The cremations and last rites performed here are believed to bring Moksha to the deceased. Liberation from the cycle of rebirth. It's already late evening, and cremations are still ongoing. We find ourselves part of these ceremonies, not as tourists but as members of the mourning families. Still, we are the only outsiders here. The heat is unbearable, though. Hats off to those who work here every day! Ashes are everywhere, and the Ganges is there to dissolve it all. Many people linger on the Ghat, either remembering their loved ones or worn out from the cremation process.

As a refreshment for everyone, we find chai vendors. Here, chai is being served in clay cups. It tastes much better. We quickly become addicted and enjoy three cups back-to-back. Let's stop at three and leave! :)

There are many more Ghats here, with the Dashashwamedh Ghat being another popular one, known for the *arti*. But by the time we arrive, it is already over, and all we see now is the waste flowers and dogs searching for food. It's okay, we can sit here, gaze at the Ganges, and let the night pass by. However, before it gets too late, we need to navigate the corridor maze to find our accommodation! :)

When we reach the hotel, we're informed that the rooms are full. Since we already booked, they're taking us somewhere else. Some place away from the main roads. No one is around. After some long walks through the maze, we arrive at a different place. Inside, there's no one here except a person dressed like a monk. The lighting is dim, the doors can't be locked, and the overall atmosphere feels shady. We have no idea what will happen next. But don't worry; we're in this together. At worst, if something bad happens, it will still be a good story. Because many people come to Kashi to spend their last days of life. We'll wait and see if this will be our last day!

Day 34

Fortunately, we are alive. Our time for Moksha hasn't come yet! :) But the time has come for the next train. Yes, we are leaving Varanasi for Patna, the capital city of Bihar. Similar to Varanasi, Patna is also one of the most continuously inhabited places in the world, home to many ancient empires and renowned scholars. We don't need to delve further into the facts because that information is easily available. However, we must admit that tracking and presenting historical information can be quite challenging. The Bihar Museum has done an exceptional job in this regard, showcasing the ancient civilizations of the Indian subcontinent in the best possible way. We often overlook the significance of history until we dig deep into it. Our appreciation for history has grown, despite once considering it a boring subject in school. What we find boring today may turn out to be interesting tomorrow. And vice versa. :)

What's harder to find, though, is the wisdom and revelations from our own experiences. That's why we are on this journey, wandering and meditating, much like Buddha did. Here we are, near to where Buddha attained enlightenment. The Buddha Smriti Park in Patna tries to recreate that nirvana experience. It's a modern, spacious, well-maintained meditation park, complete with a Buddha museum and Buddhist chants playing softly across the campus—a perfect place for meditation. So, will we attain enlightenment today? Hmm, maybe. See, "enlightenment" means achieving a greater understanding of life. It's not something that will happen all of a sudden due to some intense meditation; rather, it will occur gradually as long as we strive to understand life deeply. The more we grasp the complexities of life, the more enlightened we become. We are enlightened to some extent, then! :)

Patna seems to be growing rapidly. We see construction work going on almost everywhere, especially related to transportation and attractions, including historical landmarks like Golghar. This large stupa-style granary from the 18th century is currently undergoing renovations. Still, a lot of people come here for leisure. Some children are playing cricket, couples are posing for photos, and some girls are dancing for short videos. It's a happy place. It would have been great to climb to the top of Golghar for a panoramic view of the city, but unfortunately, the stairs are blocked.

It's evening now, but we still have plenty of time. We can visit Gandhi Maidan, a large field for recreation and events, where we can simply sit on the grass and do nothing! By the way, we are still tuned into the live evening satsang, where we're getting answers to our questions. We sent in inquiries about more sensitive topics like charity, marriage, and reproduction. Guess what? They've started skipping those questions! And that wraps up our participation. :)

Our accommodation for tonight will be the train to Siliguri in West Bengal. Surprisingly, we got upgraded to an AC coach today! In case you didn't notice, we usually travel in non-AC coaches. This upgrade is nice for the comfort it offers, but the ordinary non-AC coaches are better. The experience of feeling the air, immersing ourselves in local culture, and interacting with everyday people is far more enriching in non-AC coaches. The only advantage of AC coaches is the availability of pillows. However, we don't need them because we already have our rucksack! :)

The train departs late at night, so we still have time to kill. That's why we're heading to the Patna Marine Drive viewpoint, located beside the Digha-Sonpur Bridge, a long steel truss bridge spanning the Ganges. Marine Drive road is wide, and we see people celebrating birthday parties beside the road, complete with cake cutting, fireworks, and even bike stunts! It's not just us; many people are here to enjoy the festivities, along with numerous food stalls treating everyone well.

Reflecting on the last few places we visited, what caught our attention wasn't the attractions themselves but the people—their happy faces. Maybe we didn't find the attractions compelling enough, or maybe we weren't looking closely enough at how happy people were earlier. It's also possible we're missing that happiness within ourselves. Hmm, the last one seems like the root cause. We often appreciate happiness most when we feel its absence. And right now, we're feeling that absence a lot on this lonely journey of exploration. It's okay, though; we don't need to be happy all the time. Otherwise, happiness itself would lose its value. Life should be a mixed bag of emotions, shouldn't it? Fundamentally, we are evolved to survive, not to be happy. Blame evolution! :)

Day 35

With our journey to Siliguri in West Bengal, we officially begin the exploration of Northeast India. This region is comparatively less traveled due to limited public transportation and the absence of major cities or tourist attractions. It's going to be a different and somewhat challenging experience. For us, the primary challenge will be transportation, as there aren't many buses or trains in these northeastern areas. From Siliguri, we take a shared taxi to Darjeeling. Shared taxis are our lifeline here. The terrain is entirely mountainous, making the journey quite interesting as we pass through lush forests and tea gardens, navigating roads full of curves and bends, with picturesque valleys all along the way. This beautiful scenery continues as long as we remain in the Northeast.

As we near Darjeeling, nature takes on a different character. Everything is shrouded in heavy fog! We can't see anything beyond 10 meters, not even the lights. This is both interesting and frightening. It's interesting because it feels like natural magic, and frightening because our driver is relying on guesswork to navigate. If he misses a turn, we could easily plunge down the valley! As we gain altitude, the fog thickens, reducing visibility to just a few meters. However, it clears up in the city center of Darjeeling, which is vibrant and bustling with hundreds of street vendors, shops, and a multitude of tourists. As we stroll along Mall Road, we understand why the city is so crowded—the state-level boxing competition is happening! The back-to-back matches across all age groups are engaging, and the event is open to the public. Our timing is perfect; we can grab a bite to eat while watching the matches. We treat ourselves to some boiled corn with spicy masala, which is delicious! :)

Time flies as we watch the boxing matches. Now we understand why professional boxing attracts so many viewers and fans. However, it's getting late at night, and the crowd is starting to disperse. Today's matches are over, and our today's hostel accommodation is a few kilometers down the road. We'll have to walk; that's our only option. Along the way, we see several women selling handmade winter clothes. Just like the women we saw in Goa, these women are selling similar items. Many are watching videos on their phones, some are knitting, while only a few actively engage in selling. We can't help but wonder who will make more money and who will feel more fulfilled. Business, much like life, is all about prioritization; how we prioritize shapes the direction of our life.

By the way, our current direction is determined by Google Maps! The maps have been very helpful throughout our journey, but not today. It leads us onto a narrow path of downward steps flanked by small houses on both sides. With it being late and foggy, there's no one outside those houses. We can't see more than a few meters ahead. All we hear are dogs barking right in front and beside us. It's terrifying. We can't run because we can't see the path ahead—neither the actual road nor on the Maps. All we can do is scream for help and knock on doors. Some residents eventually come out to assist us, moving the street dogs away and trying their best to help with navigation. However, due to the language barrier, we can't fully understand what they're saying. Still, we grasp rough ideas and continue walking, only to find ourselves trapped in a thicket! We can't see anything, can't find anyone, and can't even think clearly. We're in shock—a complete shock that renders us mentally idle. We can't move much right now because there are probably harmful animals nearby. We've seen those signs in many places along the way. Don't be afraid. Let's stand still, keep calm, and try to regain our focus. Fear can transform us into someone we don't want to be. Without overcoming fear, we have no way forward. So, let's take the time to overcome that fear and bring back awareness. We can call the hostel owner and ask for help. Fortunately, he realizes we're in big trouble, explains the correct way forward, and sends someone to guide us. Thanks to him, we reach the accommodation safely. Here's to more adventures and experiences! But first, we need a deep sleep to recover from the shock! :)

Day 36

Darjeeling isn't known for its attractions; rather, the place itself is the attraction. The climate, charming cottages, vibrant markets, and scenic views of snowy peaks, tea gardens, and stunning valleys make Darjeeling a perfect summer getaway. It's no wonder the British Raj elite once considered this place a summer retreat. But since we're not here for a summer retreat, it's time to move on! We'll take a shared taxi to Gangtok, Sikkim.

What's interesting about these high-altitude trips is the hairpin bends, curvy roads, and breathtaking views. We could never get bored of it. Each hairpin bend brings a sense of deep happiness. Maybe because we can see where we came from, or maybe we simply appreciate the thrill of it. Whatever it is, it's fun! When we reflect on our achievements, we often feel happiness, don't we? The same applies here. Happiness stems from living in the moment or looking back, while motivation is about looking forward. Interesting, huh?

What's less interesting about these high-altitude trips is the traffic that arises as we enter the city. The narrow roads make it difficult for vehicles to pass smoothly, especially when we encounter trucks and buses. With the rain pouring in Gangtok, things are bound to get messier. All we can do now is wait for hours, stuck in traffic. One way to alleviate such congestion is to reduce the reliance on private vehicles whenever possible. We are doing our best in this regard, rarely hiring a cab throughout our journey. Most of our travel has been via shared transportation. Thank you for adapting!

We finally reach Gangtok by night, and it's still drizzling. The market is bustling, primarily due to the street food stalls. Momos and noodles are everywhere, with each stall packed with eager customers. How can we resist trying something delicious while walking past these stalls, captivated by the aromas? :) In contrast, on Mahatma Gandhi Marg, the main street of the city, it's less crowded. This wide walkway is lined with modern restaurants, shops, and bars, making it feel like a premium place. Not many people want to brave the rain though. For us, the rain doesn't matter. We stroll down the street, enjoying soft-serve ice cream and the ambiance, with the soothing sound of rain in the background. We can see in the eyes of many that they want to embrace the rain, but something seems to hold them back. It could be the need to maintain appearances, protect their belongings, or conform to social pressure. The first two are understandable, but the last? Nope. How can we live the life we want if we care more about how others want us to live? Being our true selves isn't just about realizing who we are; it's about living authentically. Anyway, it wouldn't be wise to spend too much time in the rain, so we should head to our hotel. Fortunately, we have an entire room tonight in a star hotel, which is good enough to dry ourselves and our clothes properly. If you're wondering how we ended up at a star hotel—it's an offer from the online booking app! :)

Day 37

Star hotels have a way of luring us in with their fluffy beds, a stark contrast to the beds we find in dormitories, lodges, and train sleeper coaches. These cozy beds tend to sap our motivation to wake up early! This is why we don't often opt for star hotels. Just kidding. :)

As we step outside to explore Gangtok, we are greeted by shared taxi drivers eager to take us somewhere. Here we go! When we commute away from the city center, we catch glimpses of ropeways and paragliding activities already in full swing. The morning has just begun, and the tourist activities are off to a lively start. The cable car glides above the main road, and it's lovely to see from below. Maybe in the next 10 to 20 years, we'll be riding in flying cars instead—who knows!

We're traveling towards Do Drul Chorten, a Buddhist temple perched on a hilltop just 10 minutes from the city center. It's near the Namgyal Institute of Tibetology, which houses a museum, library, and research center dedicated to Tibetan culture. The entire area has a distinct ambiance. No vehicles, complete silence, and a plethora of scriptures and Buddhist flags lining the path. Of course, we need to hike a bit to reach the temple.

The temple is serene, featuring a golden-domed stupa, shrines, and prayer wheels. We stroll around for a while, but what captivates us most is the prayers and rituals taking place inside the shrine. Entry is restricted, so we can only peek from the outside. Inside, about a hundred monks are seated on the floor, chanting prayers non-stop. Some monks step outside to bring in loads of soft drinks and mix them in a large container, which is then taken inside. Meanwhile, a few monks bring other containers outside and pour the mixed drinks onto the ground. What is going on here? It's a bit perplexing.

Curious, we approach a younger monk burning leaves outside as part of the ritual. He doesn't speak English or Hindi, but we persist in seeking answers. After several attempts, we learn that those thousands of liters of soft drinks are offerings to Buddha during the pooja. Once used, the drinks are poured out! Didn't expect that. We can't wait to see when this will stop, but for now, we need to leave.

As we descend from the hilltop to the next taxi stop, we pass the Black Cat Museum, a small museum run by the Army. It showcases Sikkim's history, information about past operations, impressive statues, and, of course, weapons. Almost every inhabited place has stories of struggle to tell. Is that good or bad? If we knew nothing about wars, would we worry about the next one? Anyway, right now, we need to focus on finding a shared taxi to take us back to Siliguri.

Descending now, we can see everything clearly, including the stunning Teesta River flowing alongside the roads in the valley. It accompanies us for hours on our trip to Siliguri. Speaking of the journey, eating during shared taxi trips is a unique experience. We have to eat quickly, often leaving restaurants in such haste that we sometimes forget to pay for our meal! Yes, we forgot to pay for lunch. Not good. We hand the money to the driver and ask him to settle the bill with the restaurant later, as it's one of his regular stops. Hope he does!

By evening, we're back in Siliguri with some time to spare. So where do we go when we have nowhere to be? Yes, a shrine! This time, we visit the ISKCON temple nearby. Inside, melodious bhajans are playing, and we happily listen. Music transcends language, so we become part of it everywhere. When it turns into sermons, we leave. We don't understand the language, that's why. After roaming around the temple grounds for some time, we head upstairs to read. Remember those Gandhi books we bought? We still have them with us! After our time-killing activities, we catch our train for the night, heading deeper into the Northeast. We're just getting started!

Day 38

Our 10-hour overnight train journey takes us to Guwahati in Assam. From here, we catch a bus to Shillong in Meghalaya. It may seem like a lot of travel, but it's not as extensive as it sounds. Even though these are separate states, they're small and close together, which is why there are many interstate bus services. Like our shared taxi experiences, the bus also makes a stop for breakfast. We don't want to feel guilty again for not paying for a restaurant meal like yesterday. Not this time! :)

With beautiful views of lush green hills and Umiam Lake along the way, we make our way through the small towns in the high ranges and finally arrive in Shillong. However, we have a problem: we don't have accommodation booked. We can't find any affordable stays nearby, and the fellow travelers who were with us left in their own vehicles. Despite the bus station being enormous, it's almost empty, and there's no one around to ask for help. There are no homes or anything nearby. Basically, we're feeling helpless—again! But it's okay, don't worry. Being helpless doesn't mean we've failed; it means we have an opportunity to seek help. So we explore every corner of the bus station in search of assistance. Finally, we find our savior: a staff member at the bus station. He guides us to a restaurant-cum-dormitory. It's a sketchy place, but we don't have many options. Once again, it's just us, no other guests. Anyway, let's unpack and go out.

Shillong is renowned for its natural beauty as a hill station, with its cool weather, pollution-free atmosphere, and stunning attractions. We can't miss out on these, so our first stop is Elephant Falls. This waterfall is unique in that it cascades in three steps, resembling three waterfalls combined into one. A 3-in-1 package! We start from the top and descend the steps to the bottom, following the water as it flows downward. As we climb down, when we try to zoom in and track the water, it feels like we are looking at a slow-motion version of the waterfall. The way the water hits a rock and jumps down feels so calm and mesmerizing. And when we zoom out, we witness how rapidly the water flows. Same scene, two perspectives. Interesting, right? Hmm, sometimes we need to zoom in to gain a different understanding of a subject. If we take the time to zoom into other's lives, we'll see how different they truly are. Our understanding of someone depends on the degree to which we zoom in. Wish those couples taking photos beside the waterfall would zoom in— not on their cameras, but on each other. :)

Next, we head to the Air Force Museum, a military museum showcasing models of airplanes and helicopters, air force uniforms, tools and weapons, and the history and culture of the Northeast. It's an informative and engaging museum that can spark kids' interest in these fields. For others like us, it deepens our understanding of the world. We need more museums like this! After that, there's an Orchidarium nearby, we will check it out. Not to deepen our understanding of plants, but simply to enjoy their beauty. :)

As we enter the Orchidarium, we find it completely empty except for a gardener. We have the entire orchid farm to ourselves. How delightful! The collection of orchids and succulents is stunning, featuring both indoor and outdoor plants. We're tempted to buy some of these beautiful plants, but remember we have to carry them in our rucksacks throughout the journey. It fades away that temptation.

By evening, we return to the city center. We've been able to get around these places easily thanks to shared taxis, which will stop whenever we're standing or walking on the road. Very convenient! However, the traffic near the city center is not so convenient. We find ourselves stuck in traffic for over an hour, compounded by the rain. Eventually, we reach our accommodation before nightfall. Since there are no other guests, we've got a hall that can accommodate over 10 people entirely to ourselves. Even better, dinner is served just near the bed. Wow! There's one beautiful staff member around for all the support and service. No one else anywhere nearby. Let's sit by the window and enjoy dinner. Afterward, we'll read and then sleep. Just for the record, the staff did come by to clear the plates sometime later, and nothing else happened! :)

Day 39

Even though we went to sleep yesterday with the entire hall to ourselves, we're waking up to find it crowded now. Some tourist groups, it seems. But that doesn't bother us much since it's time to leave for Sohra, also known as Cherrapunji, a small town near Shillong famous for its heavy rainfall. Getting there isn't straightforward; first, we need to reach a taxi stand, wait for a scheduled shared taxi, and then wait for more passengers to fill the nine seats. That wait can stretch up to an hour. Patience, mate! :)

Shillong and the nearby regions, like Sohra, owe their beauty to the Khasi hills. These lush green hills provide the area with its natural wonders. Root bridges, gigantic caves, countless waterfalls, and abundant rainfall. We haven't explored any caves during our journey, so today we're off to visit the Arwah Caves. Excited? Just a heads-up: it's a 2.5 km walk to get there. Simple enough. Let's go!

After reaching the entry point, we find ourselves on a lonely, rugged road. We're not sure if we're heading the right way, but we keep walking. The rugged terrain is draining our energy. We skipped breakfast and now it's already noon. Our water bottle is also empty, and there are no shops or people around to ask for help. As we hike up towards the caves, we're burning even more energy, and the hunger and thirst are becoming overwhelming. But don't worry; we'll figure something out! Luckily, we spot a small stream along the path. We don't know where the water comes from or how pure it is, but at this point, we need to drink it with gratitude. In moments of survival, all our stubbornness and ego vanish. Survival comes first, everything else is secondary. Thankfully, we have a small packet of biscuits as a backup. We settle on the grassy rocks beside the stream to drink and eat. What a feast for the starving stomach! Now, we're back on track. As we continue walking, we see a car approaching. A hired taxi with three girls and a driver. They offer us a lift, and it can save us half a kilometer of hiking. Yes, sure!

After the rugged road, we find a perfect trail with stepped paths, offering stunning views of the hills in the misty weather. Now we're encountering more people, and the trail is well-maintained and engaging. After another half-kilometer, we finally reach the cave. It's truly magical! The large rocks and fossils that form these chambers are captivating. In some places, the height of the chamber is low, so we need to keep our heads down. The rocks can be slippery, requiring us to walk carefully. But we keep exploring the limestone walls, different types of rocks and fossils, the structure of the chambers, and even the history behind them. It's worth every bit of the hike, especially on a starving stomach!

As we exit the cave and make our way back to the center of Cherrapunji, we're greeted by heavy rains. What else can we expect from the wettest place on Earth? By the way, these areas can be wonderful to live in, provided we are okay with the inconveniences that come with them. Every good thing requires sacrifice, doesn't it?

Fortunately, our timing is perfect; there's a taxi ready to leave, so we don't have to wait like we did this morning. The rain is so heavy that visibility is nearly zero, and even the taxi's roof is leaking! So now, we're enjoying the rain from both inside and outside the taxi. :) With such memorable experiences, we're leaving Shillong. We could have explored more, but traffic constraints limit our time. Also, we have an overnight bus to catch. Sit and sleep again, agh!

Day 40

We're dropped off by the bus somewhere in Silchar, Assam, early in the morning. Silchar feels more like a connecting city, and as you can expect, we're here to catch a ride to our next destination: Imphal in Manipur. After arriving at the taxi stand, we find the right people, and now it's time to start. No, not the journey, but the bargaining! There are plenty of agents and operators quoting prices up to three times the actual fare. We need to get to the bottom of this. Thankfully, we have time, as the trip to Imphal will take around 11 hours, and the shared taxis won't depart until they're full, which could take an hour or more. Yes, it's going to be another all-day travel day.

Despite the long wait, the shared taxi we finally board has only three passengers, even though it can accommodate up to eight. This gives us ample space to sit and relax, but that comfort doesn't last long. Things get tough starting from the Manipur border, where we must comply with some checks and obtain approved permits to enter the state. We didn't need permits anywhere else so far though. As we continue, the road changes drastically. It becomes rugged and jarring, shaking us continuously for hundreds of kilometers! We're traversing hilly terrains, and while there are signs of construction in some areas, the condition is still rough. Our bodies don't care about construction signs. The back pain is real! Huge respect to the drivers who endure this daily! They have things worse, too; throughout the trip, they must pay bribes at multiple unauthorized checkpoints. Anyway, we can spot at least one armed military soldier every kilometer or so. And in the evening, darkness envelops the region, leaving only the light from our taxi. This adds to the feeling that we might be getting into some trouble—beware!

By late evening, we finally reach Imphal, the capital city of Manipur. We're utterly exhausted and hungry since we only had a small meal at noon. It's getting late, so before searching for food, we need to find accommodation. Unfortunately, nothing is available online. One of our co-passengers also needs a room, so we stroll through the city together, inquiring at various lodges and hotels. After checking 5-6 places, we find a room, but we can let our co-passenger take it since he looks more tired than us.

Now, we will continue our search on our own. As we enter the markets and streets, the ambiance shifts to a sketchier vibe. We can't proceed without help from the locals, so we pop into a small restaurant to ask about nearby lodges. It's only after we step inside that we realize it isn't a restaurant but a liquor shop. Oh, trapped! We need to leave immediately, but one drunken man starts following us. Trapped again. He acts like he wants to help, but his intent quickly shifts. He grabs our hand, asks for money, and begins to threaten us. Assault! Don't be afraid. Let's think this through. There's no one around, so screaming won't help. How about using the pepper spray in our pocket? Not a good idea; we have no idea what he might have, and he could easily call his gang. Our only option is to talk things out peacefully. After several attempts, he finally releases our hand. We discreetly pull out our wallet, tuck away most of our cash, put on a helpless look, and hand him a small amount. Fortunately, he's satisfied, and we're safe now. It's our first and only time facing such an incident during our journey, and we handled it well. We controlled our fear and anger, chose the peaceful approach, and resolved it there. When we win through violence, it brings victory; but when we win with non-violence, it brings victory and peace. Well done; proud of you! :)

Even though we're safe now, we still don't feel secure. We haven't found accommodation, and the streets are getting lonelier as time passes. We remain on high alert for any further threats, which makes us nervous. In our vigilance, we forget to watch our steps. Guess what? One slab in the drainage we're walking over is broken, and we fall into the wastewater! We're now knee-deep in foul-smelling sewage, our shoes and pants completely ruined. But we have no choice; we need to keep moving until we find a lodge.

After a few more inquiries, we finally secure a room at a lodge. We still haven't eaten anything, sorry about that. For now, we'll have to make it up with our backup biscuits. Today has been one of the toughest days of our journey. Let's hope for a better tomorrow.

Day 41

It seems the Northeast cuisine isn't agreeing with us. Why? Diarrhea. Oh no! Fortunately, we have a single room in this lodge. Imagine having diarrhea in a shared room with a stranger. That would be even worse. If you remember, this isn't our first bout of diarrhea on this journey; we had it in Mumbai as well. So, what do we do when faced with this issue? Let's test our memory! We'll follow the same tactics: order stomach-friendly foods, rest, use this time to repack, wash any stinky clothes, and make some rough plans for the coming days. It's also been a while since we had a good sleep, so we'll catch up on that until the afternoon.

Diarrhea is peculiar in that it puts us in a bad condition without making us feel sick. Our minds are eager to explore Imphal, but our bodies aren't cooperating. So, we'll just stroll around the city and visit some nearby attractions. Our first stop is the Manipur State Museum, a small place showcasing the history of Manipur, some natural history sections, unique regional artifacts, and many military sculptures. The relics from the war reveal Manipur's significance during World War II.

Next, we head to the nearby Kangla Fort, the fortified palace of the ancient capital of the Manipur region. Interestingly, the fort has a moat—a real moat. You might have heard of "moat" in the context of defending a business from competition. Here, in its actual architectural form, the

Kangla Fort is surrounded by rectangular ditches filled with water for defense. Now that it's open to the public, we are not defended, we can explore inside! :)

Inside, we find large polo fields, ponds, sculptures, museums, office buildings, temples, tombs, and more. It's a spacious fort! While meditating near the pond and watching the fish, we notice a man approaching with a large plastic sack full of bread. Yes, the kind of bread we eat. But it's not for us—it's for the fish in the pond! Didn't know fish enjoyed bread as an evening snack! :) We join the man, take handfuls of bread from the sack, and toss it into the pond. Within seconds, the bread disappears upon hitting the water. The fish are clearly hungry!

After this fun activity, the fish are happy, we're happy, and the kind man with the bread is also pleased. Life is good. You see, moments of happiness often arise when we don't seek them, just for no reason at all. And when we do seek happiness, it may not always come. Happiness isn't always within our control; it's a state of the moment. But contentment is always in our control; it's a state of mind. What will you choose?

As evening approaches, let's be careful not to get into trouble like yesterday. And let's not forget—diarrhea! That's forcing us to act quickly. There's no time for caution. We better head back to our lodge soon; you know what will happen otherwise! :)

Day 42

With the unforgettable experiences from Imphal behind us, it's time to leave. Early in the morning, there's a bus to Dimapur in Nagaland, another northeastern state of India. It's home to over 15 tribes and ethnic communities—the land of the Nagas. We have two options: catch that bus or stay in Imphal for another day. Read your mind, we're catching that bus. Rush!

The journey from Imphal to Dimapur takes about 8 hours. From Dimapur, we'll catch a train to Guwahati, Assam. All planned out! So, today will be another all-day travel day. Sit tight! The bus trip offers scenic views of valleys and villages. The areas are sparsely populated, with agricultural fields, small shops appearing infrequently, and women selling fresh fruits and vegetables right outside their homes.

More interestingly, we see school-going children in their uniforms walking with parents throughout our journey. It's commendable how these parents make the effort to educate their children, despite the extra time and effort involved. In contrast, education in cities is becoming increasingly complex. There are more schools than necessary, and parents struggle to navigate the admissions process! As we progress as a society, our choices are expanding—more modes of transportation, food options, living styles, entertainment, and even relationship types. However, as the number of choices increases, decision-making becomes more challenging. Imagine if humanity had invented just one dish worldwide. Instead of fretting over what to cook or eat, we could simply enjoy that default dish. See, that's the power of fewer choices. They lead to quicker decision-making and greater contentment. But that doesn't mean we should limit ourselves to fewer options. The goal is to find a balance and optimize our actions. After all, who would want to eat the same dish every day, huh? :)

By the way, it's time to explore Nagaland's dishes. Unfortunately, diarrhea hasn't left us yet. This leads to situations where we find ourselves in the washroom while everyone else finishes eating and boards the bus. What if they leave without us? Thankfully, that won't happen. The bus and its passengers patiently wait for us. However, the train we were supposed to catch in the evening has left us due to the heavy traffic in Dimapur, which has delayed us by several hours. This is completely unexpected, meaning our subsequent plans will need to change.

It's time to rest and refresh. At least we've found accommodation nearby. We'll figure out the rest tomorrow. One advantage of these unforeseen events is that we get extra time for chores—washing clothes, repacking our rucksack, and planning transportation for the coming days. Long travels lie ahead!

Day 43

When things don't work in our favor, we often lose interest, right? It seems we're going through that phase now. We're feeling very tired and don't even want to wake up. The last few days have been tough, and it's affected our mood. Told you the Northeast would be challenging, but you didn't listen! Just kidding. :)

Traveling, especially solo, isn't always fun. It comes with a lot of anxiety, confusion, and exhaustion. It's not at all like what we see on social media feeds. When we look at the unfiltered and authentic version of things, it often doesn't seem interesting at all. Being authentic is now perceived as boring and improper sometimes, intentionally or unintentionally. If we look closely, we can see a lot of inauthenticity all around us, including the way we communicate, the decisions we make, and the lifestyle changes we embrace. The last time we wished someone a good morning or happy birthday, was it genuine, or just something we felt we had to say? Those recent decisions we made—were they purely our own, free from societal expectations? And those expensive items we bought, did we really need them? Essentially, are we living an authentic life or just the life we're "supposed to" live? The former is tough; the latter is easy. But choose wisely. :)

No matter how hard things are, we need to move on. That's life. And we need to get going now; it's already afternoon, and we're still in bed! Since we missed yesterday's train and there are no more tickets available today, we'll take a bus to Guwahati, Assam, in the evening. Until then, let's explore Dimapur. We're in the city center, the commercial hub of Nagaland.

As we walk, we find ourselves in a crowded narrow alley lined with shops on both sides. This is the Dimapur Hong Kong Market. Hundreds of shops selling clothes, electronics, food, and accessories, and thousands of shoppers bargaining and trying things on. We enter a maze filled with shops and shoppers. There are some good collections, though! It takes a while to navigate out of that maze because we have to watch the shops and the paths at the same time. :)

Dimapur is a small city, and there's not much to see. Apart from the markets, there are a few parks, churches, temples, and science centers. But we're not in the mood for any of that. We're done with this trip. Totally exhausted. If there's a bench along the road, we'd happily sleep there! Yes, that's our condition now, pretty bad. Why are you still on this journey? :) It's the hope that tomorrow will be better, isn't it? With that hope, we board the next bus. Glad we made it this far. Well done, mate. Keep it up!

Day 44

When we miss a train, it's not just about the money and time lost; it's also about the inconveniences it brings. For instance, we have to sleep on the bus overnight. If we had been on time yesterday, we could have enjoyed the comfort of a sleeper train. If you remember, we've spent nights sleeping on bus seats earlier also, but this one feels different. Maybe because we knew there was a better alternative. What if we didn't know about that option? We would have felt much better. So, does that mean ignorance is bliss? Not exactly! Most of our losses stem not from their actual impact but from the comparisons we make. Whether it's in relationships, money, health, happiness, or anything else, our inherent tendency to compare ourselves and our situations to others is the source of much of our misery. If we can master the art of non-comparison, we might find that almost all our worries fade away. And that's a tough skill to cultivate, seriously!

Anyway, our bus is on time. It's 5 in the morning, and we've arrived in Guwahati, Assam. We have a train from Kamakhya Junction nearby that will take us to New Jalpaiguri in West Bengal, by evening. From there, we'll catch another train to Kolkata. So, we're leaving the Northeast region behind. Unfortunately, our journey has turned into a bit of a train-and-bus-hopping adventure. Sorry for that! :)

But train journeys are interesting, too. The view of the Brahmaputra River from the Saraighat Bridge is breathtaking. How wide can a river be when it's full of water? For the Brahmaputra, it can be up to 35 kilometers wide, with an average width of 5 kilometers! And remember, we're talking about a river, not a lake or sea! As we pass through small villages and towns, with national parks and forests nearby, we catch glimpses of a different side of the region. We can observe the geographical and cultural changes as we travel. We gradually transition from green hills to flat plains filled with paddy fields and agricultural land, shifting from sparsely populated areas to densely populated ones. We even notice changes, such as women carrying children on their backs wrapped in clothes to carrying them on their hips!

There's a common belief that to truly understand a culture, tourists need to experience the cuisine, art forms, and festivals. While these may look great in photos, the actual ground realities are often entirely different. Those realities can be easily observed during train journeys. We prefer to see the unfiltered version, don't we? :)

Day 45

We are in Kolkata! After a long time, we're back in a metro city. Kolkata is one of the most historically and culturally significant cities in India. Very excited! Are you feeling the excitement too? Don't even think about saying you're sleepy, we had a sleeper coach yesterday! No more lethargy, no more laziness! :)

As we depart from Sealdah railway station, it's time to unpack and set out for our Kolkata exploration. Interestingly, instead of booking accommodation online, we're opting for the traditional method of finding a place offline. Dealing with hotel brokers and bargaining like real locals. We've managed to secure an affordable room with easy access to the terrace. What more could we ask for? :) It seems like offline hotel booking isn't as bad as it's made out to be.

Once we unpack and step outside, the vibrant bustle of the city hits us. The streets are alive with sellers, movers, commuters, and more. One of the most intriguing sights is the tram weaving through the crowds. It's the oldest tramway in Asia still in operation! For less than the cost of a cup of tea, we can navigate the city on these trams. With their slower pace, spacious seating, and the ringing of bells, it's a fun and unique way to travel. Unfortunately, ridership is quite low; many times, we find ourselves as the only passengers in the coach! It seems the trams have lost the popularity they once enjoyed. But it makes sense. There are metros, buses, cars, and bikes that are ten times faster. Who wants to go slow, apart from a couple of crazy people like us? :) The speed of transportation, parcel delivery, internet, careers, and even communication methods—everything is increasing. Speed has become the new measure of progress, hasn't it? Our appreciation for speed is good, as long as it doesn't become an obsession. Likewise, our appreciation for slowness is good, as long as it doesn't become a weakness. If we can optimize the speed element in our actions and daily tasks, it will positively impact our productivity without compromising our well-being.

Our first stop in Kolkata is the Birla Industrial and Technological Museum. It's scientific, informative, and inspiring. A well-managed museum filled with demonstrations and activities that spark childhood curiosity. Impactful. On a related note, curiosity, creativity, and comprehensibility diminish as we age. We can feel that if we reflect carefully! Next, we head to Science City, India's largest science park. Entering this space feels like stepping into an entirely different world. The "Evolution of Life" section takes us on a dark ride through the history of life, complete with robotic models. It's an amazing experience! And yes, there's no evolution of life without dinosaurs! The activities in the Dynamotion Hall and the exhibits in the Space and Earth sections are all fantastic. Places like this remind us how fascinating science can be, evident from the wonder on the children's faces. However, we only have limited time to explore, so it's time to move on.

From the realms of science and technology, we transition to history and politics at the Alipore Jail Museum. This over 150-year-old prison has been transformed into a museum, significant for imprisoning and executing Indian independence and freedom fighters. The atmosphere is heavy with silence, instilling a mix of fear and pride. We walk through the complex, learning about the history of Indian independence. A captivating documentary plays in one of the rooms, showcasing rare visuals and unheard stories. It's more than an hour-long video on a loop, and it draws us in so completely that we stay even as the museum begins to close. This documentary teaches us more about the history of Indian independence than years of school history classes ever could! Dear teachers and schools, please incorporate documentaries into history lessons. Students will like it! History is important. We can't understand the present and future without understanding the past. By the time the documentary ends, we find ourselves alone in the museum, with the lights dimming. Luckily, the gate is still open. Let's get out before we get trapped in jail! :)

As evening descends, we notice large crowds in the Kalighat area, with thousands of people queuing up! What's going on? We discover they are lining up to see large sculptures of the goddess Durga in beautifully decorated stages known as pandals. Today marks Durga Puja, the biggest and most important festival in West Bengal! What a coincidence! As we wander further, we encounter more pandals set up in various locations. Each more vibrant than the last, with increasing crowds, lights, sounds, and the overall intensity of celebration. Some pandals also feature live classical music performances. It seems like the pandals are competing with each other on its magnificence.

The entire city seems to come alive with festivities. It's fascinating! The energy is palpable. We're fortunate to have access to our hotel's terrace, where we can soak in the Durga Puja celebrations, from the top! The streets are bustling with vehicles and people. Friends and families enjoying the festivities, young guys attracting attention with vuvuzelas, and vendors selling an array of goods. Laughter and happiness fill the air. We are truly lucky to be here today!

Day 46

The day after a festival feels like a day off for the entire city. The roads are empty, shops are shut, and silence blankets Kolkata this morning. Luckily, the roadside chai vendors are open. Ah, it's time for some hot tea blended with spices, served in small mud cups called kulhads. This chai is the best we've ever had—so tasty that we'll be back for seconds and thirds. It's addictive! :)

Fueled by that chai energy, we set out for the day. As we check out of our accommodation, we've got our rucksack with us. You know what? We can store our rucksack in the cloakrooms available at railway stations. Yes, it's possible! It's a bit late in our journey for this realization, but it will be a great relief for the days to come! That's why we head to Howrah Junction railway station first. It's the largest, busiest, and oldest railway complex in India! The red-colored station is massive, with over 20 platforms. Surrounding the station, vendors and people are bustling about, reminiscent of yesterday's festive mood. The station itself feels like a place of attraction.

However, what truly catches our eye is the Howrah Bridge, located just near the station. It's the busiest cantilever bridge in the world, spanning the beautiful Hooghly River. As we walk toward the bridge, we marvel at its engineering marvel. The steel structure is complex and fascinating, like world-class geometric art. It's no wonder this bridge has become the icon of Kolkata. Walking on the bridge, we can appreciate the beauty of the Hooghly River. The morning sun makes the water shimmer like gold. We can't see it clearly with our eyes wide open; we need to slightly close the eyelids. Sometimes, we need to close our eyes to see things more clearly. Ideas, visions, and connections often reside within us, formed by experiences gained through open eyes. Look outward for experiences, and look inward for insights.

By the way, Howrah Bridge was renamed Rabindra Setu, in honor of Rabindranath Tagore, a prominent figure from Kolkata. This leads us to explore more about Tagore. Jorasanko Thakurbari is a museum where we could learn more about his life and family, but unfortunately, it's closed due to the festival. After a pit stop at the serene, century-old Nakhoda Mosque, we arrive at Rabindra Sadan, a cultural center. There's not much to see here either. Fortunately, we have the internet to learn about Tagore. A true polymath, respected for his diverse contributions.

Kolkata's historical significance is reflected in its architecture, with the Victoria Memorial monument standing as a testament to the British Empire. This elegant century-old memorial and museum, made of white marble, is a sight to behold. We must go inside! However, it's raining heavily, and there's a long queue for the entrance. After waiting for about an hour, we finally step inside. It's stunning. The marble sculptures, pillars, statues, domes, and spacious interiors are all breathtaking. The various galleries showcase everything from British portraits to arms to the history of Kolkata. Though it serves as a memorial for Queen Victoria, we don't learn much about her here. Instead, what stands out is the architectural brilliance and design that went into creating this structure. More than just a memorial, it feels like a statement of excellence.

After spending some time in the gardens, we make our way to St. Paul's Cathedral, which is just nearby. Another stunning creation built of marble! Though originally built as an Anglican church, its Gothic architecture makes it a popular tourist attraction. As we approach the church, we notice more people posing for photos than actually praying. It's quite captivating! :) This reminds us that just like we evolve, so do our creations, transforming into something beyond their original purpose. This applies to material creations, cultural expressions, and even our thoughts. What we value or believe today may change tomorrow. Nothing is permanent.

As the church is closing, it's time to leave. We'll stroll around the city, enjoying chai and chaat, soaking in the nightlife, and admiring the huge advertising banners put up for the festival. There's also a Birla Mandir nearby that's still open. Let's visit and spend some time there. A serene and beautiful temple, a bit removed from the city's bustle. Interestingly, the temple is also made of white marble! That's a lot of marble-watching today, haha! :)

Day 47

We find ourselves in Bhubaneswar at 6 am—up early today, not by choice but because of train timings. We can't change the train schedule to get more sleep! Anyway, we have a long day ahead to explore. Bhubaneswar is home to hundreds of ancient temples, so with the early morning light, it's the perfect time to visit some of them.

We're about to explore heritage sites with temples built in the 10th to 12th centuries! Our first stop is Kedar Gauri Park, which features the famous Mukteshwara Temple alongside a few other temples, all nestled together like neighborhood houses, each adorned with stunning carvings. The figures and designs in these carvings, from top to bottom, are marvelous! These truly are the gems of Odisha and Kalinga architecture. We could admire their beauty and the artistic skills of the creators for hours. Remember, these were built over 1,000 years ago! Here's hoping they last for at least another 1,000 years so future generations can witness the artistic marvels of the past.

Interestingly, we're the only ones here, which adds to the sense of discovery. It feels like these are hidden gems in need of more visibility. The silence surrounding the temples is complete, and beside them, we notice a rectangular pond with dark green water. Hundreds of small fish surface, and when they notice our movement, they quickly dart away to the other side of the pond. We approach the other side, and as soon as they see us again, they disappear. This playful cycle continues! It's fun. As we continue our game with the fish, time flies by, and soon, more visitors arrive. Goodbye, fishes; someone will catch you later. Pun intended, sadly.

After a quick breakfast from a nearby sweet shop, we head to the Udayagiri and Khandagiri Caves, ancient caves dating back to the 1st century BCE! Climbing up the stairs and rocks to the hilltop, we're greeted by families of langurs, jumping around and searching for bananas. It's heartwarming to see them living, caring for their young, and enjoying life. What a life they lead! If only we could enter the minds of other animals and understand their perspectives on life. Decoding the thoughts of fish, birds, animals, and other creatures might reveal insights beyond our imagination. But first, let's focus on decoding ourselves properly! :)

The caves are partly natural and partly man-made, making them an interesting attraction. We see many artistic carvings depicting various deities and scenes. The corridors, interior structures, and surrounding areas make it feel like a large dormitory within a cave. Yes, caves were once our ancestral homes, and we should be grateful for how far we've come.

From the nearby Baramunda bus station, we head back to the city center in search of the Odisha State Museum, only to find it closed. But that won't deter us! We can head to Puri, which is about an hour away. Before leaving Bhubaneswar, we must mention the Odisha thali meals. They're completely different from traditional thali meals. With so many unique dishes to choose from, we need to carefully decide what to eat. No more diarrhea days! :)

Puri is a small coastal city known for its beaches and temples, particularly the Jagannath Temple, one of the four temples in Char Dham—an essential pilgrimage site for Hindus across India. Since we have visited so many temples this morning, let's explore the beach. Upon entering the beach area, we're surprised to find an entry ticket system for beaches! Once we enter, we realize we've mistakenly accessed a private beach—the Golden Beach. With few people around, a clean shoreline, changing rooms, toilets, and other facilities, it's a perfect spot. For the first time on our journey across India, we're stepping onto a beach! Yay! It's thrilling.

The water beckons us; we're far from the shore, submerged in water up to the chest. Reaching this point in the sea involves a bit of losing balance, as the tides occasionally pull us further away. It's both frightening and exciting! There's a fine line between excitement and danger—that's the line that takes lives. And we are right there now. Do you want to step back, or take risks and go further? Taking non-fatal risks is an act of courage while pursuing clear fatal risks is pure insanity. Leaving that choice to you! :)

After a wonderful time playing and swimming in the sea, enjoying the sunset and gazing at the water, it's time to leave. To where? Another beach, haha! Yes, we're moving on to Puri Beach, the public version, which is just beside Golden Beach. As expected, Puri Beach is very crowded. What's fascinating, though, is the energy here. Stalls and vendors are selling fish, seafood, and many beach-favorite snacks. We'll try spring potatoes, masala corn, and much more. There are also plenty of sights to see: camel rides, horse rides, fishing boats, sand art, and kids playing on the beach!

While we enjoyed the sea and sunset on the private beach, here we'll soak in the sights, sea breeze, and moonlight. Hope you're happy! :) As the moonlight shines, signaling that it's late, we need to head back to the Puri railway station soon. A long journey awaits us tomorrow!

Day 48

Don't be upset, but today we'll spend the entire day on the train! Yes, it's a long journey from Puri in Odisha to Bhopal in Madhya Pradesh, covering around 1,400 km, and we'll pass through two other states:

Chhattisgarh and Maharashtra. So why are we doing this? Just to touch central India! :)

Spending one day and two nights continuously on the train means all our activities will be confined to the train, including our hygiene routines. The common toilet and basin are just a few steps away, so we can manage, even if cleanliness takes a back seat here. As more people become educated, our awareness of cleanliness is increasing, which is great. However, over-obsession with cleanliness can lead to compulsion, creating more problems down the line. Every good thing is good until it becomes obsessive!

Anyway, we won't be able to shower in the train washroom, but thankfully, we had a long session in the water yesterday, remember? Yes, that helped! As for food, there's no problem here. We can order breakfast, lunch, and dinner with plenty of choices. Numerous vendors stroll through the train, not just selling food and snacks but also personal accessories, electronics, and books! Very convenient. Oh, by the way, we still have some of those Gandhi books we bought earlier, so we can spend time reading. However, we also have a lot of other things to do: watching the scenery outside, planning for the next few days, and listening to fellow passengers. Hmm, that's a lot of work! :)

We have a window seat, which gives us better views. Along the journey, we pass through multiple cities and hundreds of villages. Most of these regions look similar, except for the changing languages. We can see lots of traditional housing, smaller scenic hills, rivers backdropping the Satpura Range, vast stretches of barren land, and large agricultural fields filled with rice, soybeans, pulses, maize, and more. Beautiful!

As we enjoy nature's beauty, two elders come to our neighboring seat: one is a teacher, and the other is a government worker. They boarded somewhere along the way. Since it's going to be a long journey and we're all sitting together, we start chatting. It's the norm, right? The conversation flows through various subjects like travel, health, pollution, sustainability, and the future of living. Both are heading to a self-sufficient community in Indore, where food, clothing, and shelter are all produced by the members using their own materials. Education, employment, and healthcare of the members are also managed by the community itself. Totally self-reliant. No imports, only exports. Appealing, huh? Yes! They are so excited about this and can't stop discussing it. They're even considering leaving their families to live in that place for years! It seems that the modern form of Sannyasa is not about retreating to forests for meditation, but rather exploring new communities for fresh experiences.

As the conversation continues, time flies, and it's already evening. Knowing we're relying on train food, the elders offer us some of their dinner! We're treated to tasty roti, an eggplant dish, and some salads. So, now we're enjoying home-cooked food from someone we just met on the train. Our trust level has grown that much!

Day 49

With 35 hours of train travel, we arrive in Bhopal, the capital of Madhya Pradesh. Known as one of the cleanest and greenest cities in India, it's also infamous for the gas leak tragedy—one of the worst industrial disasters in history. You might have heard about it in your high school classes, but if not, no worries; we'll see the site for ourselves. A 30-minute auto rickshaw ride will take us there.

You might imagine the tragedy site as a heritage location now, but it's quite different. There's no public access or entrance at all, which urges us to take shortcuts. We traverse a barren field, walk through bushy paths, and finally enter the compound of the old factory. There's no one around—just us and the ruins of the chemical plant. Old buildings, sheds, tanks, and rusty metal pipes are all covered with vines and spider webs. Everything feels abandoned. As we walk past these structures, we can visualize how they once functioned and how the tragedy changed everything, taking thousands of lives. The horror of it all is palpable as we step inside the industrial sheds. And remember, we're completely alone. After wandering around the compound for a while, we spot someone slowly emerging from a small house in the distance. Don't you feel the horror goosebumps? But wait — it's not a ghost; it's a security officer. :) He questions our intentions and asks us to leave soon. And now we see the entrance, oh no, exit!

We'll walk to the nearest housing colony, a couple of kilometers away, mainly because there's a museum here. Against our expectations, it's quite unique. A small rented house displaying pictures, stories, and facts about the disaster. It provides a clear understanding of what happened, its impact, and the lessons learned. The museum coordinators have done an excellent job of highlighting the lives of the victims and the urgent need for better safety measures. Here also, we're the only visitors, except for the caretaker, who takes our photos as we explore. Sadly, these places don't get the engagement they deserve, whether for awareness or tourism. But at least we've done our part now.

On our way back to the city, we stop to admire a 19th-century mosque, Moti Masjid. It offers a peaceful atmosphere with its beautiful architecture made of red sandstone and white marble. From the mosque's top, we get a 360-degree view of old Bhopal, including the scenic lake. Now, we're in the heart of the city, which proudly showcases its roots, history, and traditions.

To delve deeper into the culture, we visit the nearby Tribal Museum, which exceeds our expectations. It's a large complex showcasing tribal culture, lifestyle, crafts, and tools in modern, artistic ways. Life-size colorful artifacts, sculptures, and innovative models with excellent detailing make the Tribal Museum engaging for everyone. Museums should aim for this kind of combination of art and innovation to convey their purpose and spread joy.

The problem with many museums is that they dive too deep into one area without broadening their scope, which makes them less interesting. The focus on specialization can now be observed in everything. We are trained to focus on one thing from our childhood. It urges us to lock into a specific area, go deep, and find meaning within it throughout our lives. Some call it the means of livelihood, some call it the career path, and some call it their purpose or calling. But this way of living can narrow our lives, don't you think? There might be other passions and skills we would excel in if only we explored and experienced more. Expanding the breadth of life allows us to discover who we truly are and what we want. Ultimately, fulfillment comes when we combine this exploration with a righteous way of living. So, the purpose of life is to explore ourselves and pursue our interests without compromising righteousness. Simple :)

Day 50

With our overnight train journey to Hyderabad in Telangana, we're back in South India—the region from which we started. This signals that we're nearing the end of our journey, but not just yet; we have a few more days left! There's so much to see in Hyderabad itself. It's one of the most populous cities in India, and its dynamism is palpable. As we step out of the railway station, the city's rich history, culture, and growth are evident. There's a bus right beside the station that will take us directly to Golconda Fort. Why wait? Let's jump in!

Golconda is a place steeped in Hyderabad's history—a large 11th-century fort that was built and ruled by various dynasties. The fort sits atop a hill, and now it's mostly in ruins. As we enter, we're greeted by bastions, cannons, royal halls, arches, gates, quarters, and even mosques and temples! The fort's acoustic features are so impressive. Sounds made at the entrance can be heard at the top! The fort sprawls across kilometers, which means a lot of walking. As we climb the stairs to the top, we're rewarded with panoramic views of the city. The steep climb is a bit exhausting, but the legacy of the fort and its architectural grandeur mesmerize us, motivating us to go as far as we can, even if it's not all the way to the top. It's astonishing to think that people built such complex and large structures centuries ago without any advanced machinery. No wonder different dynasties sought to take control of this place. Jealousy is innate; it's one of the key driving forces behind human conflicts. That still holds true!

Our exploration of Golconda lasts until the afternoon. Afterward, we check into our accommodation and unpack. It feels great to have a full room after so many back-to-back nights of train sleeping! Our hotel is in Secunderabad, not far from the city.

Hyderabad is always bustling. It's interesting how it blends historic culture with modern development. The Nizam's Museum in Purani Haveli is a prime example. Originally a museum, it now also houses a school and college. The extensive collection of historic artifacts is fascinating. Lots of gold and silver-plated tools, equipment, utensils, and accessories. Kilos of real gold! We can also see a long hall dedicated entirely to the royal walk-in wardrobe! Imagine how confusing it must have been for the royal family to choose what to wear. Luckily, we don't have to face that hassle, haha! More choices, more trouble, isn't it?

The Sudha Car Museum offers a contrasting experience. It showcases cars and vehicles designed to resemble everyday objects, with vehicles shaped like balls, bats, cakes, shoes, cups, and even toilets! It's all quite quirky, and interestingly, most of them are functional. Can't imagine someone actually traveling in a toilet car, though! In addition to these whimsical designs, we also find many vintage cars and bikes. Historically, cars were a status symbol for the royal and wealthy families, but now they're a common possession for millions, signaling economic progress. Overall, material possessions have become easily accessible and affordable, leading to increased materialism. Unethical advertisements are one of the biggest culprits behind this trend. They play a significant role in shaping human lifestyles and values. We see many ads designed to instill insecurity, pushing us to change who we are. When this insecurity combines with FOMO (fear of missing out), it leads us to take actions that may not align with our true values and priorities. In business terms, this influences consumer behavior and drives sales. Impressive, isn't it?

By now, it's evening and many places are closing, so we head to NTR Gardens. This urban park in the city center features well-maintained gardens, water fountains, amusement activities, and plenty of resting spaces. What's particularly interesting is the view of Hussain Sagar Lake, which adjoins the park. In the lake, we can see the large Buddha statue island. We could take a boat out there, but it's better to admire it from afar. Let's spend the rest of the evening here, watching the Buddha statue glow with colorful lights, observing the construction of a new secretariat complex nearby, enjoying some street food in the light rain, and resting peacefully in the park.

Day 51

We are back in festive mode. It's Eid Milad-un-Nabi today! As we arrive in the city center of Hyderabad, the celebratory atmosphere is electric. Green flags and decorations adorn the roads, stages are set up for various events, and music fills the air, accompanied by bustling crowds and vehicles. Standing amidst it all is the renowned Charminar, the iconic 16th-century landmark that serves as the heart of Hyderabad. Despite the crowds, we manage to enter the Charminar, where we are treated to a panoramic view of the city, and the exquisite petal-like architecture of the dome.

What truly makes Charminar an icon isn't just the monument itself but also its surroundings. It's flanked by the grand Makkah Masjid mosque, the vibrant Laad Bazaar street market, historical structures like the Char Kaman, and the wide roads that all lead to it. These external factors greatly enhance Charminar's value, much like how the sun illuminates the moon, a frame enhances a painting, and context enriches a story. What we surround ourselves with has a significant impact on who we become. The people, community, environment, information, and resources that surround us profoundly influence our values, character, and actions. Additionally, the more time we spend alone, the greater our potential to discover our true selves. Solitude is underrated. Everything has its limits, though.

As we explore Charminar, festival processions begin to unfold. We can see rallies on bikes and in open jeeps, often carrying more people than the vehicles can accommodate, complete with loudspeakers attached. Large green flags are waved, and food and water packets are distributed throughout the city center. The atmosphere grows increasingly crowded, noisy, and lively. We can feel the competitive spirit among the rally participants, and after watching for a while, we find ourselves swept up in the celebration.

By afternoon, the festivities begin to wind down, and we make our way to Chowmahalla Palace, a sprawling complex of four palaces built by the Nizams. Yes, four palaces within a palace :) The palace features a large courtyard garden at its center, and inside, we're captivated by magnificent chandeliers, Persian designs, pillared halls, and repeated arches. Displays of weaponry, ornamental tools, vintage cars, and paintings offer a glimpse into the royal way of life. For royal families, luxury was inherent; it wasn't a choice. But for us now, it's completely within our control; it is a choice. We can either chase luxury or embrace simple living. The question is—what do you choose?

The festival celebrations have transformed the city's dynamics. Everything feels different compared to yesterday, with all stores, offices, and attractions closed. The Salar Jung Museum, which we hoped to visit, is also closed. So, what now? With limited options, we can take a metro ride to see the city's outskirts from above. The Hyderabad metro is elevated, providing us with great views. It may sound like a strange idea, but we commit to a one-hour round trip to Miyapur.

As we move away from the city center, we notice an increase in tightly packed housing colonies and office buildings, a pattern common in major cities. City centers tend to be more open, while the outskirts are more densely populated. This observation reinforces what we discussed earlier about the influence of our surroundings. The outskirts also shape the character of a city.

Having explored enough of Hyderabad, we feel fortunate to have experienced the festival, even if it was a coincidence. But now, it's time to leave. We have an overnight train to Visakhapatnam in Andhra Pradesh. Unfortunately, we don't have a confirmed sleeper ticket and are on the waiting list. This means we'll have to travel in the general coach. Arriving late at the station, we find that the general coach is packed, with no seats available. The only space left is on the floor near the toilet, which is also occupied. Sitting among fellow passengers, we try to make the best of it, watching a cricket match on someone's phone while glancing out the window, waiting for the next stop. As we worry about how we'll manage to sleep tonight, a new concern arises. The wash basin is blocked, the tap is leaking, and water spills onto the floor. Despite the attempts at temporary fixes with the help of co-passengers, nothing works.

We find a new spot as we sneak toward the center of the coach—a small vacant space on the floor. Many passengers of all ages and genders are already sleeping here, tightly packed. We can try to lie down as well; the floor of the train will be our bed for tonight. With the rucksack and our belongings to watch over, we can't sleep. Instead, we listen to music through our earphones, make space for others, and ensure the children around us are comfortable. Some are even sleeping on our legs now!

Day 52

Traveling in the general coach of an overnight train is more challenging than we expected. We barely managed 1-2 hours of sleep! By the time we finally get a proper seat, we've arrived in Visakhapatnam, also known as Vizag. We won't be staying overnight here, which means we have no accommodation for the day. Oh no! To make matters worse, we're feeling grimy and dirty. While we can use the public washroom at the railway station to freshen up, it's currently crowded, and we'll have to wait. It's been a rough time, so your patience during this period is truly appreciated. We've faced tougher situations before, and we'll emerge from this stronger. Maybe after the bath. :) Anyway, experiencing this train journey has certainly heightened our respect for those who regularly travel like this. When we see suffering, we tend to neglect it, but when we experience suffering ourselves, we respect it.

Vizag, known for its ancient Buddhist sites, now blends historical significance with natural beauty, modern industries, and urban development. Its fish export industry is thriving, which is why we're taking a bike taxi to the fishing harbor. As we ride through the streets, we spot local women creating beautiful rangolis at their doorsteps. It's tradition. The Kurupam Market, famous for its jewelry, is just waking up, but the fishing harbor is already bustling.

Upon entering the harbor, we're greeted by the sight of numerous fishermen, vendors, and hundreds of vibrant yellow fishing boats, all in harmony. We approach one of the boats docked nearby and observe the unloading process. They have a massive catch of squids—tens of thousands of them! The fish are loaded into buckets and passed along a human chain to the shore, where the weight is measured and recorded. This process continues as other boats unload mackerels, sardines, pomfrets, tuna, anchovies, shrimps, prawns, and more. The smell intensifies as we walk further, primarily due to the dry fish processing happening nearby. Millions of fish are laid out to dry in vast open areas— a staggering sight. The sheer volume is so immense that the occasional loss to birds and cats hardly makes a dent, and they are seizing the opportunity. Still, people are watching over the drying fish, and we see women inside sheds processing the catch, likely for export. They must have grown accustomed to the pungent odor, which is overwhelming and gives us a headache. Remember, we didn't sleep well yesterday. Before we faint, let's leave.

As a coastal city, most attractions we plan to visit are near Ramakrishna Beach or RK Beach. The long beach road is beautiful, with the clean beach on one side and well-maintained lawns on the other. Since it's around noon, the beach is relatively empty. We can stop by to enjoy some Bhel Puri chaat and sit on the rocky formations, gazing out at the vast sea filled with ships. It's a wonderful spot to sunbathe and relish the sea breeze. After this refreshing break, we're ready to explore a few museums.

The Visakha Museum features both maritime and heritage exhibits. The maritime section offers comprehensive information on naval history, navy operations, and models of warships and submarines, while the heritage section showcases statues, weapons, and historical artifacts.

We've seen so many museums, but have we ever gotten to see the inside of a submarine? Our next museum is the INS Kursura Museum, which houses a real submarine that served in the Navy for about 30 years before being decommissioned and converted into a museum. It's an incredible opportunity to see a submarine with its entire body on display. When it operates in the ocean, we only see the surface, right? Yes. But here, we can see the entire body. Inside, we can view all its organs too! :) The control systems, engines, electrical systems, navigation setups, torpedo arrangements, and more. The dummy crew members set up in the submarine quarters, kitchen, and dining area help us visualize life inside a submarine. We traverse the entire length of the vessel, marveling at how effectively the limited space is utilized. Meticulously crafted.

Now that we've seen the submarine, how about a warfare aircraft next? Yes! The TU 142 Aircraft Museum is just across the road. The Tupolev TU-142 is an anti-submarine warfare aircraft. Like the submarine, it also served the Navy for around 30 years, and we get to see inside too! Inside, we find the electrical systems, cockpit, navigation tools, engines, crew amenities, bomb bays, and even torpedoes on display. The complexity of the cockpit is astonishing, far more intricate than what we see in movies. The museum also extends outside the aircraft to explain its history, operations, and missions.

As we step out of these marvels of technology, we can't help but wonder and feel proud of human capabilities. The only problem lies in the intended use of these creations. As long as they are used for good, that's all well and good. However, if misused, they become a disgrace to the world, no matter how marvelous they may be. The value of a creation depends on the person who wields it and the purpose it's used for.

At this moment, one thing is clear: we still don't have a confirmed sleeper ticket for tonight's journey. We aim to arrive at the station early to secure a seat. Thanks to our efforts, we manage to find a seat, and we can finally rest peacefully. Goodbye, Vizag!

Day 53

We wake up at noon in Chennai Central railway station. Yes, we are in Chennai, and yes, we slept until noon to catch up on our sleep debt! Chennai Central is a century-old station, sprawling with over 15 platforms, making it the busiest railway station in South India. The energy is palpable as we step off the train. We also manage to snag a budget lodge deal from a local dealer, conveniently located within walking distance of the station. Now that we've rested enough, let's unpack and explore!

Originally known as Madras, the city was renamed Chennai only recently, and we can still see references to Madras throughout the area. Historically, during the British Empire, the first British fortress in India, Fort St. George, was established here. It became a significant trading hub, expanded over time, and evolved into the modern city we see today. Guess where we are right now? Near that very fort! Security is strict due to the official legislative buildings, but we can visit the museum inside.

Inside the museum, we find a wealth of history: numerous paintings and statues of British rulers, an impressive collection of arms and weapons, artifacts, coins, and extensive information about the city's history. Don't know if the historians will agree, but we can consider the fort a foundational element of urban Chennai. It's essential to appreciate the contributions of past regimes, even when they may seem at odds with current political entities. Before we speak against something or someone, remember that everything and everyone has a good side too :)

The fort overlooks the Bay of Bengal and serves as a starting point for Marina Beach, the world's second-longest urban beach! Before we hit the beach, we'll first visit the Vivekananda House nearby. This is where Swami Vivekananda stayed for a time, and it now features exhibits on his life and teachings. Although small, it's a well-curated museum that highlights his philosophy through quotes, paintings, statues, models, photos, and even 3D movie presentations. His emphasis on discovering inner spirituality, taking action, and maximizing our potential resonates deeply with us. This museum enriches our understanding of Vivekananda, and we can also purchase some of his books here. A worthwhile visit.

These kinds of museum visits serve as nourishment for our subconscious mind. What we consume shapes our minds, leading to varying thoughts and perceptions. This process results in new ideas, beliefs, and ways of living.

As sunset approaches, we head to Marina Beach to witness the spectacle. The beach is so vast that we can't see where it begins or ends. As we walk towards the sea, which is quite a walk, we come across numerous food stalls and vendors selling a variety of fish fry, snacks, juices, toys, clothes, and more. Let's start with some flavored sweet corn! The beach is alive with activities: horse riding, body massages, children's rides, tattooing, and, of course, people swimming and playing in the sand and waves. We find a spot on a parked wooden boat on the sandy beach to watch the transition from sunset to full moon. Many people are taking photos with the moon rising behind them. Among them is a veteran government official from Bangkok, also enjoying a solo vacation—though he has a full-time driver, which is a different experience altogether! We engage in long conversations about natural beauty, places to visit, technological advancements, and life in his country. Long conversations with lots of photo clicks in between. As time passes, the waves begin to rise and inch closer to us. We're sitting on the boat at the shore, and one wave splashes up to his hip. Is it a tsunami warning? No, don't be afraid; it's just a rise in sea level. Likely due to atmospheric pressure, tides, changing wind patterns, or something like that. Whatever the reason, it's a warning that we've been here long enough and it's time to leave. Take the hints :)

Day 54

From the floor of the train, we've now transitioned back to the comfort of hotel beds. What a relief! That relief is reflected in the quality of our sleep, tempting us to stay in bed longer. But we're not here to sleep, right? Get out of bed, right now! :)

We're heading to the Egmore railway station to deposit our luggage. Carrying a 10 kg rucksack on our backs is no easy task! We should have been aware of the cloakroom facility earlier. Regardless, since we've spent so much time on trains during our journey, how about learning more about them? There's a great place for that: the Chennai Rail Museum. It's part of the Integral Coach Factory, which manufactures railway coaches for India and several foreign countries. The rail museum itself is extensive. The indoor exhibits showcase train components, operations, models, and the history of the Integral Coach Factory. Outside, we can admire artistic works made from waste train materials, explore vintage and heritage coaches, and even ride a toy train! It's a highly informative, interesting, and joyful experience. Much more than just a museum.

What also captures our attention is the ICF Campus, which spans acres and includes residential quarters, schools, hospitals, and even electricity-generating windmills! It's fascinating to consider the impact a manufacturing unit can have on transforming a place. We should be open and welcoming to modern developments, as long as they don't harm anyone or anything. Humans tend to fear change, and our default response to new changes is often "no." Learning when to say yes and when to say no is one of the most important skills anyone can acquire. It can profoundly influence our lives, our loved ones, our community, and even the world.

Chennai is not all calm; it has bustling streets as well. Our visit to Ranganathan Street is to experience this vibrant atmosphere. The street is lined with hundreds of jewelry, apparel, and textile shops, all packed together. We're swept up in the crowd, bargaining and shopping all around us. We don't have to walk much; we'll be carried along by the rush! :) There are many more streets like this. Fascinating!

As we venture into the Pondy Bazaar area, the scene shifts. We find ourselves on wide, modern roads flanked by brand-name outlets, with fewer shoppers. Here, the sidewalks seem wider than the roads we saw earlier. This area falls under T Nagar, a premium commercial and residential neighborhood of Chennai, planned and built in a European style. Anyway, no shopping for us today! We're running low on cash. Plus, our rucksack is already full, so we can't carry anything more, which is another reasonable excuse to avoid temptation! :)

Our journey takes us back to the beachside, but no, we won't head to the beach again—just to nearby attractions. First up is the Santhome Church, a 16th-century Portuguese Catholic cathedral that houses the tomb of St.

Thomas, one of Jesus Christ's twelve apostles. It's a peaceful and serene place, and its Gothic revival architecture is stunning. The church has also served as accommodation for St. Francis Xavier during the early years of its establishment. The historic and religious significance of this church makes it a national shrine. What amazes us is St. Thomas's commitment to spreading Jesus's teachings. Who would travel to entirely different cultures and regions to preach the gospel? That requires tremendous courage, respect, and devotion.

Just a short walk from Santhome Church, we arrive at a lighthouse. The 46-meter Chennai Lighthouse offers stunning views of Marina Beach and the city. Gazing at the long sandy beach and everything surrounding it is pure bliss. We can also spot trains running frequently on the elevated tracks. From this height, everything looks so small—humans become dots, vehicles resemble matchboxes, and buildings appear as mere containers. When we zoom out, everything seems tiny and insignificant, much like our thoughts.

Fortunately, there's an elevator in the lighthouse, and our perceptions of size return to normal in seconds. Along with the tower, the lighthouse features a small museum where we can learn about the functioning of the lamp and its history through a good collection of photos, models, and equipment on display. As closing time approaches, we feel the rush to wrap up our visit.

Oh, and by the way, remember where our rucksack is? At the Egmore railway station! We have a short train journey to Pondicherry ahead of us. We'll reach there tonight, and we've even booked a retiring room. No accommodation crisis this time!

Day 55

Pondicherry is a charming French colonial city in the union territory of Puducherry, offering beautiful rock beaches, cathedrals, ashrams, botanical gardens, and more. The relaxed atmosphere of Pondicherry makes it an ideal destination for a short vacation. However, the main reason we are here is to visit Auroville, an experimental township near the city. So, we take a short morning bus ride to Auroville. However, there isn't a direct bus to Auroville, leaving us stranded about 8 km away. With no taxis, auto rickshaws, or people in sight, we set off on foot, hoping to find someone who can help us. Fortunately, we meet an architect on his way to work at Auroville, and we hitch a ride on his bike!

Auroville is essentially a community of international residents with its own governance, laws, schools, businesses, and way of living, all focused on human goodwill and unity. Spanning several kilometers, it houses over 8,000 people. At the visitor center, we gain a high-level overview of the place. To explore further, we rent a bicycle and ride around, visiting multiple pavilions such as the European Center, French Pavilion, Tibetan Pavilion, and Unity Pavilion. Each pavilion reflects its own unique culture. There are also museums and auditoriums that outline the life and principles of Aurobindo and Mirra Alfassa. As we cycle through Auroville, we pass by the residents' homes, organic farms, restaurants, and vast open fields. We're off-roading across Auroville, sometimes leaping off bumps on our rented bicycle!

After our pavilion hopping, it's time to walk toward the Matrimandir viewpoint. The trail is engaging, taking us through a forest-like atmosphere filled not only with trees and plants but also the values upheld by Auroville: sincerity, peace, equality, generosity, goodness, courage, progress, receptivity, aspiration, perseverance, gratitude, and humility. Like the petals of a flower. The walk is quite long, requiring several pit stops along the way. We discover some artistic structures that invite us to rest. Although they aren't meant for seating, we lie down and gaze up at the branches shading us, simply appreciating the beauty around us. It feels as though our minds have entered a magical state—or maybe we're just tired! Regardless, we continue walking toward the viewpoint, which offers a clear view of the Matrimandir. It's a huge geodesic dome adorned with golden discs. It is shining beautifully in the afternoon sun. Inside the sphere is a meditation chamber, though access is restricted. We can also see the twelve-petal structure that serves as the foundation for the dome.

As we return to the visitor center, we feel inspired to learn more about Aurobindo, the philosopher and yogi to whom this place is dedicated. Yes, we're expanding our spiritual book collection! The entire concept and vision of Auroville is intriguing—a world within a town embodying the goodness of humanity. Why limit such goodness to just this town? Wish it could spread further. Remember the new world we discussed earlier? We should contemplate more on it.

While getting in was challenging, leaving is easy, thanks to the kind people who offered us rides. From Pondicherry, we now head back to Chennai, this time taking a different route: the scenic East Coast Road. This straight road stretches for around 150 km, running parallel to the coastline and offering stunning views of pine trees and the beautiful beaches along the way.

One striking observation during our journey to and from Pondicherry is the significance of parallelism. We're noticing it more frequently now. Bridges, train tracks, roads, vehicles, power lines, buildings, trees, and more. Everything is parallel! See, we're constantly trying to connect the dots. This concept of parallelism inspires the idea of focusing on multiple areas simultaneously. Pursuing various hobbies, passions, careers, interests, experiences, goals, and values all at once. Essentially, it's about embracing a parallel way of living rather than a sequential one. Following multiple paths may lead to intersections, different destinations, or even dead ends. But that's progress: taking action, failing, learning, and then concentrating more on what works. Viewing life through the lens of parallelism offers a broader, harmonious, and integrated approach to living.

Day 56

Why did we return to Chennai yesterday? Did we forget or lose something? No, it's simply because we had an overnight train to Bengaluru from there. And yes, we are now in Bengaluru. Surprise! And one more surprise: our trip ends today! Sadly, everything has an end, mate.

Bengaluru is the bustling tech capital of India and the capital of Karnataka. Let's explore with no further delay. But our phone battery is dying, and we need to charge it as soon as possible. Since it's early morning, finding public places with charging stations isn't easy. But no worries! We can take a bus from the majestic Majestic Bus Stand and we can recharge the phone from the charging port on the bus. Not a bad idea, right? And where are we heading? To Electronic City. So, we're going to Electronic City to charge our phone! Interesting, huh? What matters more is what we observe along the way.

The morning hustle of the city is evident everywhere. Most people appear to be heading to work, which we can guess from their attire. The infrastructure in areas like bus stations and the outskirts is impressive, with wide roads, flyovers, and large buildings. Many of those buildings are tech offices and cafes. There seems to be an unspoken bond between the two; they're hard to separate these days!

After charging our phone and soaking in the sights, we head to the National Gallery of Modern Art, where there's a miniature painting exhibition titled "Reflections: Man and Nature in the Paintings of Bireswar Sen". Today happens to be the last day of this exhibition, and we are just lucky. The gallery features incredible watercolor paintings. But what's unique is that those painting canvases are no larger than playing cards or business cards! Most paintings depict a person wandering through mountains, waterfalls, caves, and fields, often accompanied by thoughtful words. Maybe because we relate to it so well, we can gaze at the magnificence of those paintings for hours. Some require a magnifying glass to truly appreciate their detail, which is thoughtfully provided beside the artwork. In essence, we see more in less—whether in painting or in life.

Surprisingly, there aren't many other visitors in the gallery; it's mostly just us. Artworks and exhibitions like this deserve more reach and visibility—much more than the fake news and negativity that dominate the media!

With around 8 million people living here, Bengaluru is no stranger to traffic jams, which we encounter as we navigate the city. It seems like it's an everyday experience for the residents. Anyway, we move on—toward Bengaluru Palace. A grand palace modeled after the magnificent

Windsor Castle! It boasts marvelous architecture, and spacious flower gardens, and is known for hosting major music concerts.

Inside the palace, we're greeted by high-end furnishings, vibrant paintings adorning the walls, and the audio guide explaining the history of the Wadiyar dynasty. Yet, what captures our attention most are the couples taking photos in front of the palace. At one point, a couple approaches, requesting a photo. The photographer within awakens! We ensure they get the best shots possible, even scouting for spots that capture the entire palace in the background. We should have charged them! But they kindly offer to take a photo in return. Wow, that's a first! Thank you, couple. When we politely decline, they inquire why. It's because, "If the mind can't remember this on its own, then it's not worth remembering."

Suddenly, a steady heavy rain begins to fall across Bengaluru. The elegance of the Vidhana Soudha legislative building and the lushness of Cubbon Park are now enhanced by the rain! It's a unique feeling, knowing this is our last stop. Our journey has taught us so much about life while immersing us in the richness of India. Feeling proud, grateful, and transformed. Thank you and congratulations on being part of this epic odyssey. You are awesome! Our journey doesn't end here; it continues. Until next time!

www.bjohny.com